HUMAN DIGNITY AND THE POLICE

HUMAN DIGNITY AND THE POLICE

Ethics and Integrity in Police Work

Edited By

GERALD W. LYNCH, B.A., M.A., Ph.D.

President
John Jay College of Criminal Justice

Charles C Thomas
PUBLISHER • LTD.
SPRINGFIELD • ILLINOIS • U.S.A.

Published and Distributed Throughout the World by

CHARLES C THOMAS • PUBLISHER, LTD.
2600 South First Street
Springfield, Illinois 62794-9265

© *1999 by* CHARLES C THOMAS • PUBLISHER, LTD.

ISBN 0-398-06958-1 (cloth)
ISBN 0-398-06967-0 (paper)

Library of Congress Catalog Card Number: 99-02328

With THOMAS BOOKS *careful attention is given to all details of manufacturing
and design. It is the Publisher's desire to present books that are satisfactory as to their
physical qualities and artistic possibilities and appropriate for their particular use.*
THOMAS BOOKS *will be true to those laws of quality that assure a good name
and good will.*

Printed in the United States of America
CR-R-3

Library of Congress Cataloging in Publication Data
Human dignity and the police : ethics and integrity in police work /
edited by Gerald W. Lynch.
    p.   cm.
Includes bibliographical references.
ISBN 0-398-06958-1 (cloth). -- ISBN 0-398-06967-0 (pbk.)
1. Police-community relations. 2. Human rights. 3. Police ethics
4. Police social work. 5. Police psychology. 6. Police--Attitudes.
I. Lynch, Gerald W.
HV7936.P8H85 1999
174'.93632--dc21
                                                                99-20328
                                                                      CIP

CONTRIBUTORS

JAMES T. CURRAN, M.S.W.
Dean for Special Programs and Professor,
Department of Law,
Police Science and Criminal Justice Administration,
John Jay College of Criminal Justice

ROBERT DONATO, M.A.
Lieutenant
New York City Police Department

JOHN KLEINIG, PH.D.
Professor,
Department of Law,
Police Science and Criminal Justice Administration,
John Jay College of Criminal Justice

RICHARD LOBER, J.D.
Inspector,
Florida Department of Law Enforcement

GERALD W. LYNCH, PH.D.
President,
John Jay College of Criminal Justice,
Professor,
Department of Psychology

RAYMOND PITT, PH.D.
Professor Emeritus,
Department of Sociology,
John Jay College of Criminal Justice

JAMES PLEDGER. M.P.A.
National Sales Manager,
GLOCK, Inc.

BARBARA RAFFEL PRICE, PH.D.
Dean Emerita of Graduate Studies, and Professor Emerita,
Department of Law,
Police Science and Criminal Justice Administration,
John Jay College of Criminal Justice

CARMEN RODRIGUEZ, ED.D.
Director of Affirmative Action,
Kingsborough Community College

MARIE SIMONETTI ROSEN, B.A.
Publisher,
Law Enforcement News

MARY DEPIANO ROTHLEIN, ED.D.
Vice President for Professional Development and Training,
John Jay College of Criminal Justice

STEVE ROTHLEIN, M.P.A.
Chief of Uniformed Services Division,
Metro Dade Police Department

PREFACE

This book addresses the challenging task of strengthening respect for human dignity in both the attitudes and behavior of police officers.

Article 2. of the United Nations Code of Conduct for Law Enforcement Officials, adopted in 1979, states: "In the performance of their duty, law enforcement officials shall respect and protect human dignity and maintain and uphold the human rights of all persons."

The United Nations Code focuses attention on an area of great concern worldwide, i.e., how the police treat the people whom they are employed to protect and serve. This book was inspired by a course on human dignity that has been offered to hundreds of police officers in Latin America, the Caribbean, Central America, eastern Europe, and the United States. The widespread interest generated by the course, and continuing public concern about police abuse of authority, suggest that publication of the insights gleaned in the process of developing a training program to prevent police misuse of their authority would be of value.

The guiding theme of the book is that integrity in police work is essential to viable and effective law enforcement. The question of how to oversee and control the behavior and actions of police is, of course, central to this issue. Not only must police recognize the fundamental dignity of all, but they must develop and adhere to high ethical and professional standards.

This work is important because it addresses a critical issue for society which, to our knowledge, has not been solved in any country in the world—that is, the enormous challenge of how best to control the police and eliminate misuse of authority and excessive force against citizens by their police. The reader will acquire a thorough understanding of the problem of police misuse of authority and the dangers inherent to a society where an absence of a sense of a human dignity on the part of the police is the norm.

In addition to articulating the dangers of police abuse, the book points to positive and effective steps that can be taken to begin to change the culture of policing through carefully constructed, appropriate training and individual officer development. At the same time, the book makes clear to the reader that training is only part, albeit a very necessary part, of the answer and that other safeguards—administrative, legal, public scrutiny—must also be in place and continuously functioning.

G.W.L.

ACKNOWLEDGMENTS

This book centers around the concept of human dignity as an innate right of all human beings. While many are intellectually committed to the universal dignity of each person, far too often the actions of human beings against one another belies this commitment. Recorded history is replete with examples of violations of human dignity committed against individuals, as well as against entire national, ethnic, or religious groups. Tragically, but expectedly, these violations are most often committed by those who hold positions of authority.

My work, for the past thirty years, has focused on the education and professionalization of police officers, and on the study of the role of police in society. Development of the "Human Dignity and the Police" course has been one of the most challenging and rewarding experiences of my professional career.

The idea of writing this book came when I realized that "Human Dignity and the Police," developed and implemented at John Jay College of Criminal Justice, was having a profound impact on all who participated in it, including the course designers, the trainers, and the participants.

As an educator, I felt obliged to share this remarkable teaching/learning experience with others. While over the years, the premises, methodologies, and results have been presented at academic and professional conferences, nothing had been provided for the larger audiences, including students, who were not able to attend these oral presentations. Thus, this book.

No list of acknowledgments is ever complete. At the outset, I apologize for any omission of people who made this work possible, because so many provided ideas, insights, and constructive criticism. On the other hand, I would be remiss if I did not acknowledge those individuals and organizations that have been committed to the idea and ideal of human dignity and who have worked very hard in making the course "Human Dignity and the Police" a reality.

I would therefore like to acknowledge the work of the late David "Kris" Kriskovich, FBI Bureau Chief and Special Agent, Director of ICITAP. Kris was the inspirational leader who helped launch the Human Dignity course and the friend and colleague to whom I have dedicated this book.

Special acknowledgment belongs to James Curran. It was his insight that lead us to understand how we could draw police officers into the personal and vibrant processes that make the Human Dignity course unique and successful. In addition, Jim has been the tireless director of the Human Dignity course training. In this effort, he has the support of an outstanding administrative team, led by Debra Hairston Parker, assisted by Valerie Jairpersaud, and at earlier program stages, by Rosemary Corres and Ahalia Lekhram.

A great deal of credit for the success of the "Human Dignity and the Police" program also goes to those who developed and piloted the original version of the course: John Bergman, George Cockburn, James Curran, Sonya Delgado, Tom Fernandez, Alan Goodman, John Kleinig, Barbara Price, Carmen Rodriguez, Mary DePiano Rothlein, and Mike Rowan.

My sincere appreciation also to Ray Pitt who, as senior trainer and training coordinator, serves in the dual role of lead course trainer and trainer of other trainers who have conducted the course; and to Julio Hernandez-Miyares, Robert Donato, and Carolyn Tricomi-Higgins who are senior trainers who worked initially with Dr. Pitt but now lead training teams themselves.

Also very important to the program are McKee Anderson, George Cockburn, Carmen Solis, Evelyn Garcia, Seymour Jones, and Bob Louden who serve as trainers in the Human Dignity program. Important, too, are Don Goodman, Cheryl Fiandaca, David McCauley, and Gregory Thomas who served on training teams for the New York City Police and Correction Department Trainers and for New York City Police Cadets.

Everyone involved in the Human Dignity program also appreciated the research and editorial and manuscript preparation work provided by Yolanda Casillas, Ahalia Lakhram, Mayra Nieves, John Taveras, Kathy Willis, and Marchelle Yoch, and especially Kathy Willis for her dedication and professionalism

Several federal agencies evidenced their belief in and support of human dignity as an essential component for policing in democratic

societies by including John Jay College in various international training programs. I especially thank FBI Director Louis Freeh for inviting
John Jay College to participate in the cirriculum development for the
International Law Enforcement Academy in Bedapest and in supporting the emphasis on human dignity in this program. These agencies
include the Federal Bureau of Investigation, ICITAP, the Treasury
Department's Federal Law Enforcement Training Center and the Drug
Enforcement Administration. The support of these agencies enhanced
the credibility of the concept of human dignity among professional
police agencies. We thank them.

The creative, rigorous and painstaking work that went into the
Human Dignity course development and preparation provided the
basis for this book. I want to thank each of the authors for their
thoughtful contributions, with special appreciation to James Curran
and Mary DePiano Rothlein who oversaw the project from start to fin-
ish. Mary Rothlein sustained each of us in organizing the book, edit-
ing chapters, and following through on deadlines. She and Jim Curran
worked wonders not only in developing the curriculum but in bringing the story of "Human Dignity and the Police" to life in this book.

Lastly, I want to thank the hundreds of law enforcement officials
who participated in the course. These professional women and men
provided a bountiful source of challenging ideas and inspirational
insights into the future of policing a democratic society.

CONTENTS

Page

Preface   vii

Chapter

1. HUMAN DIGNITY AND THE POLICE: BACKGROUND AND   3
   DEVELOPMENT OF THE IDEA
   Gerald W. Lynch

2. HUMAN DIGNITY AND HUMAN RIGHTS: AN EMERGING   8
   CONCERN IN POLICE PRACTICE
   John Kleinig

3. POLICE AGENCY EFFORTS TO PREVENT ABUSES   15
   Steve Rothlein

   Arthur McDuffie
   The Rodney King Incident
   The Christopher Commission
   Michael Dowd
   Civilian Review
   Conclusion

4. GOVERNMENT RESPONSE TO POLICE ABUSE OF POWER   28
   Richard Lober

   Federal Efforts to Halt the Indignities Suffered at the Hands of
   Local Police

5. THE ROLE OF THE PRESS IN POLICE REFORM   34
   Marie Simonetti Rosen

   The Police Perspective
   The Press Perspective

6. COURSE DEVELOPMENT AND EVOLUTION 49
   James T. Curran and Mary D. Rothlein

   Background
   Need for The Human Dignity Course
   Training Methodology
   Humanistic Philosophical Basis
   Input from Participants: Adults Must Actively Participate In
      Their Own Learning
   Overview of the Course

7. THE EXPERIENTIAL APPROACH: THE ROLE OF THE 61
   TRAINER AND ITS CRITICAL IMPORTANCE
   Raymond Pitt

   The Training Program
   The Program Exercises
   The Final Exercises

8. THE COURSE AS A CHANGE AGENT: IMPACT ON 75
   INSTRUCTOR AND IMPACT ON PARTICIPANTS
   Carmen Rodriguez

   Introduction
   A Brief Overview of Transformative Learning
   The Course

9. HUMAN DIGNITY AND THE POLICE: A PRACTITIONER'S 86
   VIEW
   Robert Donato

10. HUMAN DIGNITY AND THE POLICE: A HUMAN RIGHTS 91
    COMPONENT OF THE INTERNATIONAL LAW
    ENFORCEMENT ACADEMY
    James Pledger

11. IMPACT AND IMPORTANCE OF HUMAN DIGNITY 98
    TRAINING FOR EMERGING DEMOCRACIES IN THE
    NEWLY INDEPENDENT NATIONS OF EASTERN AND
    CENTRAL EUROPE
    Gerald W. Lynch

12. ISSUES TO BE ADDRESSED IN EVALUATING THE HUMAN 104
DIGNITY TRAINING PROGRAM
Barbara Raffel Price

    The Interactive Survey
    End Of Course Evaluation Questionnaire
    Follow-Up Interviews

13. THE FUTURE: WHAT IT WILL BRING? WHAT MUST WE DO? 111
Gerald W. Lynch

Appendices
A. Human Dignity and the Police: Morality, Integrity, and Professional 121
    Ethics in Police Work
B. Report on the June Workshop: An Electronic Interactive Survey of 145
    Police Officials from South and Central America and the Caribbean
    on the Subject of Human Dignity
C. International Law Enforcement Academy Session Evaluation Data 150
    Summaries
D. An Assessment of the Impact of the Human Dignity Course 155

Bibliography 159
Index 164

HUMAN DIGNITY AND THE POLICE

Chapter 1

HUMAN DIGNITY AND THE POLICE: BACKGROUND AND DEVELOPMENT OF THE IDEA

Gerald W. Lynch

The question, "Who guards the guards, who polices the police?" is one that cries out to us nineteen centuries after the Roman poet Juvenal (AD 60-140) asked, *"Quis custodiet ipsos custodes?"*

We expect a high degree of professionalism and integrity from our police and expect them to perform in an exemplary manner, every time we call on them. We admire them for their gallantry under fire and the heroic sacrifices that they make in protecting us. On the other hand, we resent any intrusion they may make on our lives (especially if we feel they are using their authority excessively or unnecessarily) and we are quick to complain about any curtailment of our freedom.

One of the fundamental purposes of government, as it states in the Preamble to the United States Constitution, is "to preserve domestic tranquility." Simply put, no society can maintain its civilization for very long without the rule of law. And no society can maintain law without law enforcement. The ability of a society to enforce its laws and protect its citizens requires a professional police force. Such a police force must always be strong and powerful enough to suppress violent and criminal behavior. At the same time, it must be tempered and responsive enough not to lose control of the power that it has been given. Walking that fine line, somehow meeting those two responsibilities, constitutes the great challenge of the police in a democratic society.

3

Over the past fifteen years, the U.S. government has been sharing its law enforcement expertise with police departments in the emerging democracies of the Caribbean and throughout Central and South America. The training is conducted by the State Department and the Department of Justice under the auspices of the International Criminal Investigative Training Assistance Program. (This is referred to as ICITAP and pronounced Issey-tap.) In countries throughout Latin America and the Caribbean, from Honduras, Peru, and Jamaica to Guyana, St. Lucia, and Colombia, ICITAP has succeeded in creating high-level training programs to the acclaim of national police agencies, ministries of government, and the oversight committees in the U.S. Congress.

It is essential that police under the emerging and the new democratic regimes demonstrate that they can maintain order and public safety. It is equally essential that they demonstrate that this can be done <u>without</u> violating human rights. The development of democratic institutions in these societies thus depends in large part on how well their police are able to organize themselves around the principles of fairness and humane treatment.

The director of ICITAP from its inception until his retirement was Kris Kriskovich, a veteran FBI agent. Under Kriskovich's leadership, ICITAP succeeded in developing police training programs tailored to the needs of emerging democracies. These programs included a wide range of "how to" courses, including courses on homicide investigation, interviewing suspects, and police administration. ICITAP had not, however, addressed the underlying, fundamental issues of professional policing with all this concept implies: respect and protection of the human dignity of each person.

In 1994, I met in Washington with Kris Kriskovich and Richard Roth, special assistant to then Attorney General Dick Thornburgh. Among other things, they described in depth how ICITAP's work had progressed to the point where they were prepared to address directly, in a specially developed course, the overall quality of the relationship of police to the people they serve. Problem areas, including abuse of power, physical coercion, brutality, and corruption were some of the issues that such a course would address. As I boarded the plane to return to New York, I pondered the question of how a forum could be created in which police officers would seriously discuss these very sensitive, gut-wrenching issues.

Kriskovich was even more specific about the curriculum, insisting that the goal of the course should be to inculcate in the participants a respect for "human dignity" rather than "human rights." "Human rights," he explained, was often the catchphrase used by the U.S. and other Western governments to criticize the internal policies of many Third World nations, and officers might associate the term with being lectured to or treated in a condescending way. Moreover, within these countries, the term was usually associated with the cases of poor people who had run into trouble with the law and protested their mistreatment. Either way, employing the term "human rights" might likely provoke negative reactions. But "human dignity," he believed, was regarded internationally as a positive and inclusive term. (The United Nations Charter in its Preamble, for instance, refers to "fundamental human rights in the dignity and worth of the human person."[2]

The plane ride back to New York ushered in a long, arduous struggle to develop a course to address the many ethical issues of police work. The challenge was to convince police officers to open up to each other in a classroom setting and freely exchange their views and feelings. I was also acutely aware that the Human Dignity course would be taught in countries and cultures different from our own, and that particular sensitivity would be required.

From the beginning, "Human Dignity and the Police" sought to imbue police practice with a heightened understanding of human dignity as an innate quality possessed by all people. To some, that might sound like a rather lofty and impractical concept. But we were very conscious that in societies which had no tradition of constitutional restraint on power, no precedent of proper police procedure to follow, and strong peer and cultural pressure to resort to violent or authoritarian methods, a program such as this might well make the difference in determining whether democracy would be able to sustain itself and take root.

After consulting with faculty and administrators at John Jay College, we eventually arrived at the conclusion that the best approach for introducing the "human dignity" concept would be to adopt a truly evocative, interactive approach. This method sought first and foremost to ask questions that would form the basis of the beginnings of productive discussion.

---

[2] Charter of the United Nations Preamble

We drew on research on how adults learn best and incorporated participants' personal experiences in order to get them involved and committed to the course. We then applied the skills of teachers, therapists, group leaders, and facilitators to encourage participation, openness, and frankness. However, while we felt secure in the effectiveness of this approach, we also knew that this method would create a challenging new problem.

ICITAP's prior courses had been mostly didactic training courses. The educational modality was an instructor providing information to students who were expected to master the facts. There was little or no analytical component. For example, in discussing patrol functions or crime scene investigations, there was a thorough body of knowledge which was usually presented in a traditional teaching format.

With the Human Dignity course, we were asking ourselves to step away from this form of clear, direct transmission of information, and instead to raise with the students a host of ethical and moral questions on the role of police in democratic societies. This kind of self-reflection is important for all police and is especially relevant in emerging democracies where the police are struggling to become independent of the military establishment to which they either reported directly or indirectly.

Over the first year, we consulted with many faculty members from John Jay and with other experts in the fields of philosophy, ethics, and group dynamics. Together we sought to find the appropriate structure for eliciting maximum participation so as to have the greatest impact on the course participants.

As the course has developed over a period of time, it now aims to achieve a broad range of objectives:

1. To have the participants so imbued with the innateness of human dignity, that it impacts on their personal and professional attitudes and behavior.

2. To encourage participants to ask soul-searching, important questions.

3. To enhance participants' own human dignity.

4. To make the course experience exciting and dramatic.

5. To make the experience free-flowing so that as in all successful enterprises, the outcome appears to be natural.

6. To draw upon the talents and experiences of a diverse group of scholars and law enforcement professionals.

7. To bear in mind, as the course organizers, that the course is never a completed work. It is a continuous process, an extraordinary opportunity, an unfolding mystery, an intelligent and compelling story which is modified and adapted to by each participant, group, country, and culture.

In an institution, certain events emerge that are especially timely. This course signified such an event. John Jay College was into its early maturity, just nearing its 30th anniversary when we undertook this ambitious project. We had been dealing with the issues pertaining to ethical policing for many years. For example, John Jay College requires every undergraduate student to complete an "ethics" course as well as a course on "race and ethnicity." The College publishes both a quarterly scholarly journal, *Criminal Justice Ethics,* and the biweekly national newspaper, *Law Enforcement News.*

The course, "Human Dignity and the Police," gave to those who developed it the unique opportunity to condense and distill what we teach throughout an entire semester into an intensive examination of ethical aspects of policing in a democratic society.

Over time, we have established some guiding principles in support of those aims. We have found it essential, wherever we go, in whatever country or culture we teach the course, to talk about the concept of "human dignity" in an intensive way. For the course to be considered a success, our discussions regarding police behavior, training, and administration should lead to meaningful actions in the way that police officers and police agencies deal with the general public. For the officers who participate, the course should seek change not only their perception of daily police work but their entire worldview.

The chapters that follow describe the many facets of "Human Dignity and the Police"—its thoughtful and thought-provoking discussions, its lively interactions, its intensive role-playing exercises. Like all worthy educational endeavors, the course is constantly changing to meet new challenges. As of May 1999, the course has been conducted in more than two dozen languages for police officers from a wide variety of cultural, religious, and ethnic backgrounds.

Chapter 2

HUMAN DIGNITY AND HUMAN RIGHTS: AN EMERGING CONCERN IN POLICE PRACTICE

JOHN KLEINIG

As early as 1961, there were calls for the United Nations to sponsor an international code of police ethics, but it was not until 1975 that a committee was set up to draft such a document—and it took another four years before the General Assembly finally adopted its Code of Conduct for Law Enforcement Officials in December 1979 (Kleinig with Zhang, 1993, reprinted with historical annotations, pp. 97-102). Consisting of eight articles and associated commentaries, the Code is intended to provide a framework that can be implemented wherever the police function is to be found.

Article 2 of the Code states:

> In the performance of their duty, law enforcement officials shall respect and protect human dignity and maintain and uphold the human rights of all persons.

It is a significant statement, citing the respect and protection of human dignity above all, and then linking human rights to this idea. Why put "human dignity" first? What is the relationship between dignity and human rights and should it be necessary to make such a statement in the first place.

Article 1 helps explain why:

> Law enforcement officials shall at all times fulfill the duty imposed on them by law, by serving the community and by protecting all persons against illegal acts, consistent with the high degree of responsibility required by their profession.

Police officers are almost always government officials, sworn to uphold and enforce the law. This seems innocent enough when viewed within the framework of a vigorous, working democracy. But where "serving the community" means maintaining the power of an incumbent dictatorship, where "protecting all persons against illegal acts" means the enforcement of discriminatory laws, and where the "illegal acts" people must be protected against are, in fact, the struggles of the oppressed against illegitimate authority, law enforcement can be easily corrupted into something other than the honorable profession it was intended to be. Thus, Article 2 is there to reinforce Article 1, and to guard against its misinterpretation or misuse.

There was a reason why the United Nations drew up its Code of Conduct when it did, and why the Code is worded the way it is. Throughout the 1970s, and well into the 80s, many countries, including quite a few U.N. member nations, were ruled by regimes that maintained themselves in power by using their police and military establishments to suppress their own populations. The Code of Conduct, though it was only a collective statement of will, made a point. At the time of its adoption, far too many nations fell below even the minimum standards of professional police conduct that it enunciated.

Recent years have seen dramatic changes–in Africa, South and Central America, eastern Europe and the former Soviet Union. Old regimes, some colonial, some of more recent vintage, have increasingly succumbed to the weight of their own oppressiveness. It has been a turbulent time for some countries as new generations have sought to overcome the enforced ignorance of the past, and reorder the social lives of their people, while vestiges of the old order have sought to hang on to power.

Against this background, it has become particularly important for the police agencies of these countries to transform themselves from agents of the old regime into genuine servants of the people–to go from being an occupying army to functioning as true peacekeepers. The Code of Conduct recognizes this with specific stipulations that any use of force by police must be necessary and proportionate (Article 3), that privacy and confidentiality must be respected (Article 4), that torture may not be used (Article 5), that the medical needs of those in custody must be acknowledged (Article 6), and that corruption in the ranks must not be tolerated (Article 7).

Article 1 of the Code also refers to "the high degree of responsibility required by their [police officers'] profession." There may be reasonable areas of disagreement over what the professional status of a police officer should be, but there is no dispute about the need for police officers to act in a professional manner at all times. It is certainly reasonable to expect police to have a professional ethic—to demonstrate an acceptance and understanding of what their work requires of them, and a dedication to meeting those requirements to the best of their ability. To the extent that police officers take to heart the need for professionalism, they will tend to acquire for themselves a set of attitudes that work against the many temptations and pressures that have traditionally compromised and corrupted police work. That, in fact, is the basic intent and thrust of the Code of Conduct—that its provisions will be internalized by police throughout the world, rather than being seen by them as an arbitrary yardstick to which they must adhere. But mere professionalism is not enough. Charles-Henri Sanson, the official executioner of the French Revolution, was a dedicated professional, constantly concerned about how he could improve the quality of his work. But the task to which Sanson dedicated his career was embedded in a dangerously shallow conception of his social role, with the result that he could, with equal "professionalism," serve whichever side sought his expertise (Applbaum, 1995). For the performance of police to be a credit to their profession, policing must be seen and understood as a service to the people. Thus are they, and we, expected to interpret the United Nations Code.

At the time the "Human Dignity and the Police" initiative was in its planning stages, much discussion centered on whether the course should focus on police recognition of human "rights" over the acknowledgment of human "dignity." Some of the discussion was tactical: the United States had invoked "human rights" as an ideological weapon in its dealings with other nations, and any use of this language in a training program overseas could well be viewed as yet another attempt at U.S. "hegemony." But there were deeper issues as well. "Rights" talk has a tendency to be divisive and adversarial: I assert my rights against others. In societies burdened with a history of oppression, still fragmented by suspicion and dominated by elites, where any burgeoning sense of community was still fragile, the rhetoric of "rights" was not likely to have the desired healing effect. It was important to connect with the police, not alienate them; what was needed was vocabulary that would sensitize officers by embracing them.

Thus "Human Dignity and the Police" was consciously structured by its creators to conform to the philosophy that had been articulated by the international community itself through the United Nations Code of Conduct for Law Enforcement Officials. Rights were not to be ignored or denied, but recourse to them should be through communally recognized channels. It is by virtue of our shared dignity as human beings that we can acknowledge others, and be acknowledged ourselves, as bearers of rights. What we claim as our rights—that we be granted certain fundamental liberties of thought, belief, and expression, that we be secured against invasions of our person and home—arise out of our standing as beings with an inherent dignity. Those rights are not ends in themselves; they are the social and legal conditions through which our dignity is maintained.

The decision to focus on the joint initiative between John Jay College and the U.S. Department of Justice on "Human Dignity and the Police" seems especially appropriate when we take a deeper look at the roots of the word "dignity," as writer Elizabeth Maclaren (1977) did in an essay in the *Journal of Medical Ethics.* According to Maclaren, the Latin word *dignitas* originally had elitist connotations, betokening "gravity, sobriety, steadiness through changing circumstances, the capacity to retain [one's] pride, balance in the cultivation of one's mental and physical powers" (p. 40). We can still see the residue of this understanding of the word when people are said to "carry themselves with dignity" and when someone is referred to as having an "expressive sense of dignity," or "speaking with great dignity" or "behaving in a dignified manner." But the *dignitas* that went with being a member of an elite, Maclaren suggested, was eventually superseded. Under the influence of Judeo-Christian egalitarianism, the creation of human beings in God's image—and God's indiscriminate love for each, whatever the individual's station in life—was taken to invest every person with dignity.

It is this second, universalized understanding of "human dignity," born in Christianity but nurtured within the spreading secularism of the 18th century Enlightenment, that has become the centerpiece of liberal, democratic humanitarian aspirations. Its most influential intellectual proponent was the rationalist philosopher Immanual Kant (trans. 1963), 1724-1804, though earlier precursors such as Giovanni Pico della Mirandola (trans. 1956; Dales, 1979), 1463-1494, laid some of the conceptual groundwork. It was Kant's contention that within human society, everything is accorded a price or a dignity. Things with a price may be exchanged for some equivalent, but things to which a "dignity" is accorded are "exalted above all else and so admit of no equivalent." Human beings, Kant believed, inherently possess dignity. Their persons cannot be substituted for one another, nor can they be traded for some other value—not power, not pleasure, not even the good of society. The Caiaphas Principle—that it is better for one person to die than that the people themselves should perish—mistakenly assumes that the value of human lives can be aggregated, Kant argues, but human beings possess a dignity that places them beyond any such aggregation (John 11:50). And, by the same token, each individual has a claim against the demands or ambitions of others. Raisons d'état do not qualify as grounds for the use of excessive force, torture, or manipulation.

For Kant, as for most thinkers who have subsequently defended dignity as a general human attribute, it is by virtue of our power to reason that we humans possess dignity. Our capacity to frame for ourselves the choices we make, the paths we tread, and the goals we pursue is an innate quality we share with other human beings, giving all persons equality of standing.

This means, in Kant's words, that we must always be treated as "ends," and never as a "means" by others to achieve their own ends, however high-minded those ends might be. Thus was born Kant's concept of the categorical imperative: "The dignity of man consists precisely in his capacity to make universal law, although only on condition of being himself also subject to the law he makes." To the extent that we interfere with the dignity of others—with their ability to control their lives, to form friendships and families as they please, to make their own choices of careers to pursue and organizations to join—we undermine the basis for our dignity. If we attempt to justify our control over others, we in turn justify the proposition that others can have control over us.

Kant's view of human dignity drives the United Nations Code of Conduct for Law Enforcement Officials, as can be clearly seen in its specific injunctions.

Article 3, for example, makes clear that force may be used by police officers only when it is "strictly necessary and to the extent required for the performance of their duty." Officers may not use more force than is needed, or more force than is proportionate to the offense for which the person is being apprehended. Use of unnecessary or excessive force violates human dignity by subjecting the person against whom the force is used to the will of another without legitimate reason.

Article 4, with its requirement to respect privacy and confidentiality, recognizes that the nature of police work often makes officers privy to matters that are private. But human beings need privacy if they are to be able to conduct orderly social relations. Additionally, private information that police may obtain could be used against an individual. This is why, as the accompanying Commentary to Article 4 makes clear, disclosure of such information is justified "only in the performance of duty or to serve the needs of justice."

The clearest link between the United Nations Code's definition of "human dignity" with Kant's classic formulation of the categorical imperative is to be found in Article 5, with its absolute prohibition against "inflicting, instigating or tolerating any act of torture to override rational judgement, to use pain and suffering and fear so that someone else will give information or make statements they would not otherwise have done. And it is the inevitable result of torture that a human being is degraded, demoralized and dehumanized, literally reduced to the level of an animal, by other human beings."[1]

Article 6, which seeks to "ensure the full protection of the health of persons" in custody, and immediate medical attention where it is needed, is likewise consistent with the historic philosophical basis behind the concept of human dignity. It is incumbent on law enforcement officials that they never permit an interruption of someone's social and legal freedom (by being arrested or jailed) to compromise that person's basic autonomy as a human being through illness, disease or injury.

At first glance, the injunctions against corruption in Article 7 might not appear to have a connection with "human dignity" concepts; corrupt police officials, after all, seek to use their authority for selfish gain rather than to gain unjust power over others. However, corruption inside law enforcement agencies has ramifications that are no less corrosive to the underpinnings of "human dignity" than the other failings to which police officers are prone. The public trust vested in officers,

---

[1] The flipside is aptly captured by Samuel Johnson: "Whatever withdraws us from the power of our sense; whatever makes the past, the distant or the future, predominate over the present, advances us in the dignity of thinking things" (*Journey to the Western Islands of Scotland,* 1775).

that they will carry out their responsibilities impartially and enforce the law without favor, is intended to sustain a social order in which people may conduct their lives with some predictability, in a state of official legal equality. Corruption subverts that trust and that social order, disturbing the tranquility that should go with domestic peace. Human dignity, though it is ours at birth as individuals, is nonetheless sustained collectively through communal mechanisms, such as law. Corruption of the law thus distorts the entire environment in which "human dignity" can flourish.

Through its Code of Conduct for Law Enforcement Officials, the United Nations sought to uphold and foster the idea of "human dignity" by police throughout the world. It did so not by setting aside its long-standing commitment to human rights, made in its 1948 Universal Declaration of Human Rights[2] and other documents, but by acknowledging that such rights have a deeper rationale embedded in the international recognition of human dignity.

In creating the course, "Human Dignity and the Police," John Jay College of Criminal Justice followed the path the United Nations Code of Conduct had laid out, and put those ideas into practice, in the actual face-to-face training of professional police officers.

REFERENCES

Applbaum, A. (1995). Professional detachment: The executioner of Paris. *Harvard Law Review, 109*(2), 458-486.

Dales, R. C. (1979). A medieval view of human dignity. *Journal of the History of Ideas, 38*(4), 557-559.

Kant, I. (1963). *Groundwork of the metaphysic of morals.* (H.J. Paton, Trans.). New York: Barnes & Noble. (Original work published in 1785).

Kleinig, J. with Zhang, Y. (Comps. & Eds.). (1993). *Professional law enforcement codes: A documentary collection.* Westport, CT: Greenwood Press.

Maclaren, E. A. (1977). Dignity. *Journal of Medical Ethics, 3,* 40.

Pico della Mirandola, G. (1956). *Oration on the dignity of man.* (A.R. Caponigri, Trans.) Washington, DC: Regnery Gateway. (Original work published in 1496).

---

[2] Article I of the 1948 Universal Declaration of Human Rights reads: "All human beings are born free and equal in dignity and rights." Although neither the Universal Declaration nor the Code of Conduct explicitly ground human rights in human dignity, there is in these and other documents a consistent ordering of the two that suggests some priority for the former. Ironically, the preoccupation with human rights (to the neglect of dignity) has usually resulted in the attempt to ground human dignity in human rights rather than vice versa. For discussion, see Michael J. Meyer, "Dignity, Rights and Self-Control," *Ethics,* XCIX, 3 (April 1989), pp. 520-34.

Chapter 3

POLICE AGENCY EFFORTS TO PREVENT ABUSES

Steve Rothlein

As soon as law enforcement agencies began to develop in the United States, the challenge of ensuring public safety and maintaining order in a free society void of police misconduct began to emerge. Similar to the airline crashes and the recovery of the "black box" recorder to avoid future aviation errors, law enforcement has review boards, commissions, and other agencies to handle this function. These groups serve to discover how police misconduct is able to permeate an agency, and sometimes even multiply within that agency. While there is no "black box" *per se*, some of these commissions have provided valuable insight, explaining what practices allowed corruption to flourish, as well as providing proactive steps which can be taken to minimize future problems.

This section will briefly highlight some of the more significant commissions established in the past, discuss the issue of civilian review boards, and acquaint the reader with a few misconduct cases which have altered the path of law enforcement. The willingness to acknowledge mistakes and to examine past failures is the first step toward professional law enforcement. In order to understand how to develop more dignified behavior from police officers, one must pay attention to the studies which followed some of law enforcement's biggest failures.

Perhaps the first major commission ever established to review police misconduct in the United States was the **Wickersham Commission** in 1931. President Hoover established this Commission which published a 14-volume report on criminal justice in America. One volume was specifically dedicated to a review of police practices and emphasized the need for training and upgrading police service. A second volume was devoted to examining police brutality—the use of third-degree tactics in order to secure confessions and even torture as a means of gaining compliance (Kappeler, Sluder, & Alper, 1994).

> The third degree brutalizes the police, hardens the prisoners against society, and lowers the esteem in which the administration of justice is held by the public. (Skolnick & Fyfe, 1993, p. 43)
> - National Commission on Law Observance and Enforcement,
> George Wickersham, Chairman, 1931

The report shocked the conscience of the American public as dramatically as the Rodney King Incident did almost 60 years later. Law enforcement agencies became very defensive and attempted to justify their behavior. The International Association of Chiefs of Police (IACP) established a committee to refute the Commission's allegations (Kappeler et al., 1994).

In the 1940s, the public was focused on World War II and police corruption did not receive the attention of the previous decade. Nonetheless, there were instances that grabbed national attention. Police in Los Angeles were accused by a grand jury of protecting prostitutes for $100 per week apiece. A racial riot in Detroit left 34 dead and cost 2 million dollars in property damage. The police were criticized for failing to properly handle incidents involving racial violence (Kappeler et al., 1994).

In the 1950s, police corruption again came to the forefront. The public watched the televised hearings of the **Kefauver Committee** which exposed extensive corruption in government. Grand juries were impaneled in Oakland, California and Philadelphia, Pennsylvania to examine allegations of payoffs and extortions. The 60s and 70s were decades in law enforcement history when most scholars would agree that the public and the government began to seriously consider the delivery of police services and the need for professional standards (Kappeler et al., 1994).

Five blue-ribbon national commissions were formulated during this period to examine the practices of law enforcement agencies and make recommendations for reforms (Municipal Management Series, 1991).

• The President's Commission on Law Enforcement and the Administration of Justice—1967, 1968.

• The National Advisory Commission on Civil Disorders (Kerner Commission)–1967.

• The President's Commission on the Causes and Prevention of Violence–1968.

• The President's Commission on Campus Unrest–Kent State–1970.

• The National Advisory Commission on Criminal Justice Standards and Goals–1973.

The most significant exposé on police corruption in the 1970s may have been in **Knapp Commission Report on Police Corruption**, published in 1973. This report took a serious look at institutional corruption in the largest police department in the country. Appointed by New York City Mayor John Lindsay in 1970, the Commission took a bold stance in identifying corrupt practices of gratuities, organized payoffs, and corruption throughout the organization. Frank Serpico, a detective who testified about corruption at the hearings, was portrayed in a book and a blockbuster movie. This raised the awareness of the general public concerning police corruption.

The Knapp Commission examined the issues of accepting gratuities and described the slippery slope leading to corrupt practices. The report that was generated was a significant exposé on the code of silence that allowed institutional corruption to flourish in the New York City Police Department.

The Report described corrupt police behavior as follows:

> Corruption, although widespread, is by no means uniform in degree. Corrupt policemen have been described as falling into two basic categories: "Meat-Eaters" and "Grass Eaters" ...The meat eaters are those policemen who ...agressively misuse their police powers for personal gain. The grass eaters simply accept the payoffs that the happenstances of police work throw their way. (Delattre, 1991)

The Commission described five major factors which influenced how much graft an officer received and the source of the gratuities. These were:

1. The character of the officer which is the primary factor and determines whether an officer would accept any gratuity or what level of graft he would accept.

2. The officer's unit or particular branch of the department. Plainclothes vice assignments provided more opportunity to become involved in payoffs.

3. The officer's geographic area of assignment. Harlem, for example, was known as "the Gold Coast" because of the vice activities which were considered to be lucrative graft opportunities by the officers receiving payoffs.

4. The officer's specific assignment. Assignment in uniform to police sector cars was considered to be lucrative compared to a dignitary protection assignment at city hall.

5. The last factor the Commission identified was rank. The higher the rank, the higher the expected amount of payoff that was expected.

During the next two decades, numerous police misconduct scandals erupted from coast to coast which sparked police reforms to combat this misconduct. Two incidents which will forever leave their mark in the quest toward police professionalism are the Arthur McDuffie case in Miami, Florida, and the Rodney King incident in California. Each was followed by substantial reforms to prevent future abuse by the involved law enforcement agencies. The implications of these watershed events are substantial and will positively impact upon law enforcement in general for generations to come. The following is a brief review of each incident and the major recommendations for change which resulted.

ARTHUR MCDUFFIE

In December 1979, Arthur McDuffie, a thirty-three-year-old black insurance executive, went for a late night ride on his motorcycle. After committing a traffic violation, he refused to pull over when a Metro-Dade police officer attempted to stop him. McDuffie led numerous officers on an 8-mile, high-speed chase and was subsequently apprehended. What transpired following his capture would lead to the most destructive riot in United States history prior to the Rodney King incident. Numerous Anglo and Latin Metro-Dade officers were accused of beating McDuffie to death and then conspiring to cover up the beating. They reported that his injuries were the result of his losing control of his motorcycle at the conclusion of the chase. The medical examiner was able to establish that he was savagely beaten with a metal flashlight, and several officers eventually came forward and testified about the beating and the ensuing cover-up.

Five officers were indicted for manslaughter and evidence tampering while several others were fired for administrative violations. The trial was moved to Tampa, Florida, because of the intense media coverage and a request for a change of venue. The Dade County community fully expected a conviction based upon the extensive media coverage and the testimony by other officers that the beating, in fact, had occurred. The black community described the incident as another lynching and were demanding and expecting justice.

On May 17, 1980, an all white jury acquitted all of the defendants of all charges. By 9:00 p.m., Miami's Liberty City exploded with widespread looting and savage beatings of white motorists. The National Guard was activated and, for the next nine days attempted to restore order to the community. Before it was over, the police recorded 1,400 arrests, 18 deaths, and damage was estimated to be in excess of $125 million dollars (Skolnick & Fyfe, 1993).

Following the verdict, the city simmered and the police and the community struggled to understand what led to this violent disturbance. Clearly, the McDuffie verdict was the flashpoint which ignited tensions that were escalating for a long period of time in Miami. The U.S. Department of Justice (1980) analyzed police activity before and after the disturbance and issued a report for the Law Enforcement Assistance Administration entitled, *Prevention and Control of Urban Disorders, Issues for the 1980's.* The report in part stated:

> Although deep-seated anger, frustration and disappointment with the role of the police and the criminal justice system in Dade County were not the sole causes of the disorder, few would disagree with the judgement that action or inactions by the police contributed to and aggravated the potential for violent outbreak." (*The Miami Herald*, 1980, p. 1B)

The Metro-Dade and Miami Police Departments failed to recognize the potential for violence in the aftermath of the verdict and were not prepared to handle a civil disturbance of this magnitude.

This report focused not only on the McDuffie case but also provided valuable insight into assessing tension between the police and the community in order to better anticipate the potential outbreak of a civil disturbance. The report suggested certain indicators of unrest which should be used to gauge the "State of Community Mental Health" between the police and the citizens they serve. These factors include:

• Disturbance calls involving conflicts between groups.
• Incidents in which the responding police officer finds him/herself the target of abuse over what is considered routine police action.
• Incidents of stoning of police or fire vehicles responding to calls for service.
• Assaults between groups.
• Assaults against police.
• Citizen complaints of excessive force by police officers.
• Changes in media coverage of police events or incidents.
• Lack of citizen willingness to assist police in routine matters.

In their book *Above the Law*, Skolnick and Fyfe (1993) cite the Metro-Dade Police Department as rising from the ashes of this disturbance into an outstanding police agency. The Department created **Citizen Advisory Committees** at each district station to assist in formulating policies. At the same time, the Department implemented an ambitious affirmative action program in recruitment and promotional standards. The **Metro-Dade Police/Citizen Violence Reduction Project** was also implemented to enhance officers' skills at diffusing violent confrontations. Every officer in the Department completed the training which included a series of role playing exercises and, according to Project Director J. Fyfe, use of force and complaints against officers dropped between 30 and 50 percent in the following year and a half.

Another important program evolving from this distrubance is the **Field Force Concept**. The Field Force Concept of response to civil disturbance became a major component of training for both the Metro-Dade and Miami Police Departments to better prepare personnel for mobilization of resources. Several minor disturbances in the mid 1980s were contained as a result of the Field Force Concept. On January 16, 1989, Miami Police Officer William Lozano shot a black motorcyclist which resulted in a 3-day civil distrubance. The Field Force Concept proved a significant success in containing the disturbance to a relatively small area.

THE RODNEY KING INCIDENT

In the early morning hours of March 3, 1991, a California Highway Patrol officer observed a vehicle being driven by Rodney King traveling at a high rate of speed on the 210 Freeway and attempted to initiate a traffic stop. The motorist fled in the vehicle and a pursuit began which lasted almost 8 miles and ended at Foothill Boulevard with a total of 27 officers on the scene. George Holliday, a local resident, was awakened by the sirens and, from his apartment, began to videotape the apprehension of Rodney King. The 90-second videotape that he produced will be remembered as one of the most significant events in law enforcement history. Rodney King was struck 56 times and shocked twice with a tasser gun as he was surrounded by officers. The national and international community was shocked as the tape was repeatedly played around the world on CNN news (Skolnick & Fyfe, 1993).

Four LAPD officers were charged with a variety of crimes involving brutality against Rodney King. The officers were tried in Simi Valley, California, an affluent community, and on April 29, 1992, the nation heard the verdict. Like Miami, the city of Los Angeles erupted in flames when not guilty verdicts were returned against three out of four officers. The jury hung on one count against the fourth officer. Before the ensuing disturbance was over, sixty people were dead, two thousand injured, and damage was estimated to exceed 800 million dollars (Koon & Deitz, 1992). While a second trial in federal court resulted in two officers being convicted, the LAPD continues to struggle to regain the confidence of many of the citizens whom it is mandated to serve.

THE CHRISTOPHER COMMISSION

In addition to the investigation being conducted by the Los Angeles Police Commission and LAPD Internal Affairs section, the Mayor of Los Angeles appointed an independent commission to review the Rodney King incident. Warren Christopher was selected to head the **Independent Commission on the Los Angeles Police Department** (1991) to examine all aspects of the LAPD which contributed to the problem of excessive force. The panel raised questions concerning the LAPD, specifically:

• The apparent failure to control or discipline officers with repeated complaints of excessive force.

• Concerns about the LAPD's "culture" and officers' attitudes toward racial and other minorities.

• The difficulties the public encounters in attempting to make complaints against LAPD officers.

• The role of the LAPD leadership and civilian oversight authorities in addressing our contributing to these problems.

The Commission reviewed departmental files and extensive data which revealed that a relatively small number of officers were responsible for a substantial portion of excessive force complaints: of approximately 1,800 officers, against whom an allegation of excessive force or improper tactics was made from 1986 to 1990, more than 1,400 had only one or two allegations. But 183 officers had four or more allegations, 44 had six or more, 16 had eight or more, and one had 16 such allegations.

The Commission noted patterns of racism and bias which became evident in their review of the Mobile Digital Terminal (MDTs) messages sent between patrol units. Pervasive failure of supervisors to monitor and act on these transmissions was noted by the Commission.

The final report illuminated concerns with recruitment, training, supervision, the complaint process, and numerous other areas in which the Los Angeles Police Department clearly needed substantial improvement. The publication of the report has allowed other law enforcement agencies to better understand how the King incident happened and perhaps to inspect their own organizations to ensure that safeguards similiar to those recommended by the Christopher Commission are in place.

MICHAEL DOWD

On May 6, 1992, Suffolk County police officers arrested NYPD Officer Michael Dowd for serious narcotics trafficking charges. Embarrassing questions began to surface as to why, after 13 previous complaints to NYPD about Dowd's misconduct in 10 years, another police department was responsible for effecting his arrest. NYPD Sergeant Joseph Trimboli publicly acknowledged that he had investigated allegations against Dowd for five years, but he believed that high-ranking members of the Department "Did not want this investigation to exist. They wanted it to go away" because they feared another embarrassing scandal "like what had occurred in the 77th precinct ...." (Independent Commission of the Los Angeles Police Department, 1991, p. 50).

Commissioner Lee Brown directed that a departmental inquiry be conducted following Dowd's arrest to determine why the department's investigative apparatus failed. The department noted a number of deficiencies but as the corruption scandal in Dowd's precinct widened, the public demanded answers as to the measures being taken to cleanse the Department of widespread corruption.

In July 1992, New York City Mayor David Dinkins signed an executive order which created **The Commission to Investigate Allegations of Police Corruption and the Anti-Corruption Procedures of the Police Department** (commonly referred to as the Mollen Commission).

Milton Mollen, a highly respected judge, was selected to chair this commission which was given a threefold mandate:

• To investigate the nature and extent of police corruption in the New York City Police Department.

• To evaluate the Police Department's procedures for preventing and detecting corruption.

• To recommend changes and improvements in those procedures.

The Commission (1994) issued an extensive report which exceeded the initial mandate, detailing the new character of police corruption. Michael Armstrong, Chief Counsel to the earlier Knapp Commission, may have summed up the new state of modern police corruption best when he testified at the Mollen Commission on October 7, 1993:

> The crooks, however, that you have uncovered, the criminals seem to be a different breed of criminal [than twenty-years ago], ... the guys you're digging up, these guys are walking around with lead-lined gloves and riding shotgun for organized crime people, it seems to me they have changed the nature of being a "meat eater" in the Department. Instead of taking money to look the other way while someone else commits a street crime, they're out there competing with the criminals to commit street crimes themselves, and it seems to me that is a very big difference. (p. 22)

The Mollen Commission boldly exposed widespread corruption in the NYPD involving activities such as drug-trafficking, theft, burglary, robbery, perjury, and the use of excessive force to facilitate corruption.

The Commission's recommendations to prevent corruption and enhance the investigative capabilities of the internal affairs process sounded an alarm to law enforcement agencies nationwide. The failure of the NYPD to apprehend Officer Michael Dowd, prior to his arrest by the Suffolk County Police Department, was symptomatic of an internal monitoring system that was almost totally dysfunctional.

As in many other law enforcement agencies, internal affairs units in the NYPD were not given the resources, personnel, or equipment to effectively investigate and expose corrupt behavior within the organization. The Mollen Commission highlighted the importance of prioritizing the internal affairs process as a signal to all agency members that integrity control is high priority. The recommendations of this Commission have become a valuable asset to all law enforcement agencies concerned with combating the new breed of police corruption which has surfaced in the 90s.

CIVILIAN REVIEW

In light of the sensational incidents of police misconduct which have surfaced during the last half of the century, the issue of creating the best system to investigate the police themselves has emerged. Douglas Perez (1994) completed a 15-year study of police review systems throughout the United States. His book, *Common Sense About Police Review*, is perhaps the most comprehensive analysis of this topic ever compiled and provides valuable insight on the issues involved.

Traditionally, law enforcement executives and police union officials have desperately resisted attempts to involve civilians in the investigation of police misconduct. They argue that this process reduces morale and cannot be effective because civilians do not have the training or investigative expertise to properly handle this function. They further argue that civilians will tend to disregard officers' rights and cater to the emotions of the press and the community when a scapegoat is needed to ease tensions.

Advocates of civilian review argue that police cannot be trusted to investigate their own personnel. These advocates contend that police internal affairs investigations sustain few allegations of misconduct. They further argue that civilian personnel outside the involved agency are more objective and diligent in reviewing allegations of misconduct. Many even suggest that civilian review will validate complaints more often and reduce police abuses. The research conducted by Perez cuts through the emotional debate and provides a basis to judge the pros and cons of civilian review. This is a tremendous value to communities confronting this issue. Perez indicated that there exists over 30 variations of civilian review mechanisms in the United States. He notes that of the 25,000 law enforcement agencies, all but a few have some type of internal review process for investigating police misconduct. The most significant findings in Perez' study can be summarized as follows:

1. Internal affairs units sustain misconduct on average 25 percent of the time. Civilian review agencies sustain misconduct on average 10 percent of the time.

2. Citizen complainants and witnesses are more comfortable with civilian investigators.

3. Police witnesses and subject officers tend to be more open with police investigators.

4. Where cities have parallel civilian and police controlled internal systems, no significant difference in the outcome of cases exists.

5. Police internal systems are clearly harder on themselves, than their civilian counterparts.

A national survey of the 50 largest cities in the United States, published by the University of Nebraska at Omaha in 1991, disclosed the recent popularity of the civilian review process as indicated in the following text: "sixty percent of the fifty largest cities in the United States have a civilian review process. Fifteen, half of the current total, have been established since 1986" (Walker & Bumphus, 1991).

The oldest continuously operating civilian review board in the United States is the Berkeley Police Review Commission (PRC). The board was founded in 1973 and runs parallel to the departmental internal review system operating in Berkeley. Perez (1992) noted that while perceived as effective by the citizens, it is expensive to maintain since it operates in addition to the system already in place in the Berkeley Police Department. Almost a half million dollars annually to investigate 100 complaints in a city of 104,000 people is a major drain on the municipal operating budget, especially when these same complaints are already being investigated by the police department itself.

The issue of civilian review will continue to be debated for generations to come. In the 1990s, as the spirit of community policing continues to reinvent the dynamics of law enforcement, police administrators will continue to explore how best to embrace the concept to involve civilians in the complaint-investigation process. The critical issue in this entire dynamic is one of trust. Police misconduct is often investigated by internal affairs, the local prosecuting authority, the U.S. Attorneys Office, the FBI, the Civil Rights Commission, grand juries, and numerous other agencies. No matter how comprehensive and impartial these investigative bodies are, the perception of some in the community will be that government is not capable of policing itself. The philosophy of community policing clearly establishes citizen participation and involvement in all departmental issues of community concern. As the wave of community policing continues to sweep the country, civilian review will evolve as a major component of effective law enforcement. The essential ingredient to validate the process is the involvement of the community itself via some form of civilian review.

The cornerstone of "Human Dignity and the Police" must be grounded in the element of trust. No matter how thorough, impartial, and objective a departmental internal affairs unit is, the public will never completely trust the police to recognize the need to involve civilians at some level in this process to establish the necessary credibility with the public.

CONCLUSION

Almost since its inception, law enforcement in the United States has struggled to balance the need to maintain public order and provide police services without violating citizens' rights and basic human dignity. Historically, the enormous power and authority granted to individual police officers to protect citizens has led to numerous scandals of brutality and corruption throughout the country.

Beginning with the Wickersham Commission in 1931, the preceding discussion highlighted a few of the sensational police misconduct scandals. In each case, commissions were established to help prevent future problems. The Knapp Commission, the Christopher Commission, and the Mollen Commission have all published extensive reports which illuminated the reason why the respective police departments failed to prevent the misconduct.

The issue of civilian review has emerged as a component in the process of rebuilding the image of law enforcement. The work of Douglas Perez, discussed in this section, demonstrates that while police undoubtedly are capable of policing themselves, civilians must play a role in the process to maintain credibility with the public.

Law enforcement, as a profession, will always have individuals who will abuse their power and authority. The challenge each agency faces is to identify unsuitable individuals early in their careers and to replace them with individuals who have strength of character to function in the complex and demanding world of police service.

REFERENCES

Delattre, E. J. (1991). *Character and cops: Ethics in policing* (3rd ed.). Washington, DC: ICMA.

Kappeler, V. E., Sluder, R. D., & Alper, G. P. (1994). *Forces of deviance: Understanding the dark side of policing.* Prospect, IL: Waveland Press, Inc.

Koon, S. C., & Deitz, R. (1992). *Presumed Guilty.* Washington, DC: Regnery Gateway.

Los Angeles, CA Independent Commission on the Los Angeles Police Department. (1991). *Report* (Summary). Los Angeles, CA.

Municipal Management Series, Local Government Police Management (3rd ed.). (1991). Washington, DC: ICMA.

New York City Mayor's Commission to Investigate Allegations of Police Corruption. (1973). *The Knapp Commission report on police corruption.* New York: George Braziller.

New York, NY Commission to Investigate Allegations of Police Corruption. (1994). *Commission report.* New York, NY.

Perez, D. W. (1992). Police review systems. *Management Information Service, 24*(8), 1-15.

Prevention and control of urban disorders: Issues for the 1980's. (1980, October 27). *The Miami Herald,* p. 1B.

Skolnick, J. H., & Fyfe, J. J. (1993). *Above the law: Police and the excessive use of force.* New York: MacMillan Free Press.

U.S. Department of Justice, Law Enforcement Assistance Administration. (1980). *Prevention and control of urban disorders: Issues for the 1980's.* Washington, DC: University Research Corporation.

Walker, S., & Bumphus, V. W. (1991). Civilian review of the police: A national survey of the 50 largest cities. *Criminal Justice Police Focus, 91-93.*

Chapter 4

GOVERNMENT RESPONSE TO POLICE ABUSE OF POWER

RICHARD LOBER

R ecent generations can conjure up vivid images of police misconduct which evoke a sense of disgust at the apparent trampling of
the civil rights of the citizenry: police dog attacks and beatings of black
protesters in the South during the civil rights movement of the 1960s;
nightstick assaults and tear gas attacks of Vietnam War protesters by
the Chicago police in the 1960s; and brutal beatings of suspects in custody, such as Rodney King in the 1990s, have been captured on video
for the evening news.

Each of these incidents has ignited calls for government response
such as independent investigative commissions, civilian review, or
separate federal investigations by the Justice Department. Often, there
is a public outcry for some independent entity to investigate and prosecute those accused of wrongdoing. The community has been left with
the feeling that their local police agency is incapable of policing itself
and that such violations of rights have become institutionalized by the
very police who are sworn to protect them. No longer having faith in
the system, the victims of such abuses, community activists, or local
leaders have sought federal intervention to right the wrongs of the
local police. This recent call for federal intervention to "police the
police" raises questions concerning the constitutionality of federal
efforts to halt the indignities suffered by some at the hands of local
police.

FEDERAL EFFORTS TO HALT THE INDIGNITIES SUFFERED AT THE HANDS OF LOCAL POLICE

The use of federal civil rights laws and federal law enforcement to protect the "human dignity" of citizens from the abuses of local police runs counter to the original intent of constitutional protections established by the founding fathers. Yet it is the use of such civil rights laws and the judicial expansion of the constitutional protections afforded thereunder that have filled the void perceived by the public in local police departments' ability to police themselves.

The rights, protections, freedoms, or human dignities which are most often infringed upon by police misconduct are those established by the Constitution of the United States. In particular, the Fourteenth Amendment to the Constitution guarantees that "No person...be deprived of life, liberty, or property, without due process of law." However, in creating these rights, the founding fathers did not envision using federal military troops to enforce them. "The new Constitution proposed in 1787 met with opposition on several grounds; but no feature was more controversial than its provision for a national army, even though the army's maintenance was to be at the discretion of the legislature, exercised at least every second year (Art. I sec. 8, cl.12). The specter of military suppression of disorders had not lost its horror" (Rowe & Whelan, 1985, p. 4).

A delicate balance needed to be established in the new federal form of government. Such a balance could only be achieved by clearly leaving matters of state or local concern to the control of the states. Ensuring the safety of the people from local threats, such as crime, or disorder and enforcement of laws established by the states fell clearly within the province of the states. Local law enforcement was a local responsibility, not the responsibility of a federal military which was constitutionally established to protect the people from foreign threats (Rowe & Whelan, 1985).

Unlike many of the European countries which had a national police agency to conduct law enforcement activities in the particular country, the United States adopted a law enforcement model similar to that of England (Cole, Frankowski, & Gertz, 1987). Many of the criminal laws and procedures in the United States evolved from the common law in England (Cole et al., 1987). So also was the English tradition of allowing for local control of police matters brought across the Atlantic.

However, the colonists' experience with the King's use of the English military to maintain local order was fresh in the minds of the drafters of the Constitution. They held in disdain the use of British troops to control the colonists at the expense of their freedoms and liberty (Rowe & Whelan, 1985). Constitutional delegates were well aware that use of the newly formed federal military in local matters would be perceived with no less disdain than was the use of British troops to suppress the activities of American colonists.

In establishing a clear line of demarcation, the Articles of Confederation and the Constitution spoke loudly and clearly in denouncing any centralized efforts to intervene in matters of local law enforcement (Rowe & Whelan, 1985). Having just won independence from the King's army, the founding fathers were passionate in their resolve that state or local matters of law enforcement be left to the state, county, or city. Nowhere in the Constitution was there any reference to the authority of their newly established federal government to create or maintain a federal police force or to conduct law enforcement activities in the states (Cole et al., 1987). Such language was deliberately excluded in order to obtain ratification of the Constitution by the state convention delegates.

With such an antifederal law enforcement fervor, it was nearly a century before any significant developments occurred in relation to federal intervention in matters of local law enforcement. The Civil War and its aftermath provided an opportunity to revisit the question of federal intervention. Congress acted without concern for the delicate balance of federal versus states rights and passed sweeping legislative reforms in the form of the Civil Rights Act of 1871 which was designed to "protect individuals against misuse of power" by the states which had previously claimed their sovereignty over local matters (*Jones v. Marshall*, 1975, p. 132). This shift from maintaining "a delicate balance" to employing federal authority to address local deprivations of a person's civil rights has evolved with judicial support. "In an unbroken line of Supreme Court cases...the conduct of police officers and other state officials has, both civilly and criminally, been held subject to standards demanded by the Constitution of the United States, regardless of approbation by state law. This is necessarily so because one of the principal purposes underlying the Civil Rights Acts of 1871 and 1875 was to protect individuals against misuse of power possessed by virtue of state law and made possible only because the wrongdoer is cloaked with the authority of state law" (*Jones v. Marshall*, 1975, p. 137).

Federal civil rights law evolved to curb the types of government abuses which most infringe upon the rights and dignity of the people, that is, the abuses of a person's basic civil rights at the hands of those government servants who have sworn to uphold and enforce the Constitution and the laws of the land. According to the Report of the United States Civil Rights Commission (1981), false arrest, false imprisonment, assault, battery, and wrongful death exemplify the types of police misconduct which led the victims of such abuse to seek legal redress against those responsible. Civil suits initiated in the state courts were the most common avenue of redress for victims of police abuse. Mistrust of local police, prosecutors, and inability of state courts to protect their rights have, however, forced many victims to turn to the federal government to right their wrongs.

The federal statute which is principally relied upon to protect the constitutional rights of those who have fallen victim to police misconduct is 42 U.S.C. section 183 (1979), which states:

> Every person who, under color of any statute, ordinance, regulation, custom, or usage, of any State or Territory or the District of Columbia, subjects or causes to be subjected, any citizen of the United States or other person within the jurisdiction thereof to the deprivation of any rights, privileges, or immunities secured by the Constitution and laws, shall be liable to the party injured in an action at law, suit in equity, or other proper proceeding for redress. For the purposes of this section, any Act of Congress applicable exclusively to the District of Columbia shall be considered to be a statute of the District of Columbia.

This federal civil action provided redress for the victims of police abuse, but plaintiffs were initially limited in the kinds of relief available to them. Judgments rendered against individual officers did not usually result in changes to the police department's abusive practices which were symptomatic of institutional police misconduct. Police departments claimed immunity from civil liability or a lack of responsibility for an officer's individual acts of brutality. By rebuffing these civil claims, the police departments or municipalities left an unmistakable impression on victims and the local community that acts of police abuse were either tolerated or would remain unchecked. There were deficiencies in the use of federal civil claims to adequately remedy local police practices of abuse.

Some of these deficiencies were addressed in the judicial arena. Under certain circumstances, victims of police abuse can seek damages not only against the involved officers but also against the municipality when officers actions carried out a policy, ordinance, regulation, or official decision of the local government entity. Further examples of the expansion of a victim's redress under the federal civil rights statutes included the improper use of force by police during an arrest (60 ALR Fed. 204); imposition of liability for the failure of supervision and the failure of police departments to train, supervise, and control officers who violate a person's civil rights (70 ALR Fed. 17); and liability which even reached a police officer's off-duty misconduct (56 ALR Fed. 895).

Civil redress for violations of a person's constitutional rights provides only a partial solution to local police misconduct. Such litigation is costly and time consuming and usually only serves the direct interest of the victim of police abuse. Public outcry for relief from police corruption cases involving civil rights violations, increased media exposure, and community awareness often calls for more immediate action to punish the offending officers and deter others from such illegal practices. In such instances, federal law enforcement agencies, such as the FBI and the Justice Department, can become directly involved in policing the police. 18 U.S.C.sections 241 and 242 (1988) are the principal criminal civil rights statutes used to prosecute local police for civil rights violations. Section 241 makes it unlawful to conspire to deprive a citizen of his/her civil rights and section 242 makes it a criminal offense for a person who "...under color of any law, statute, ordinance, regulation, or custom, willfully subjects any inhabitant of any state, territory, or district to the deprivation of any rights, privileges, or immunities secured or protected by the Constitution or laws of the United States."

Federal criminal prosecutions for police misconduct go directly to the heart of protecting public safety and the dignity of citizens as guaranteed by the Constitution and federal civil rights laws. On its face, use of a federal law enforcement agency to police the local police seems inconsistent with the original intent of the framers of our Constitution to maintain separation of federal authority and state law enforcement authority. But it is apparent that the evolution of the federal government's role to investigate, prosecute, punish, and thereby to deter police misconduct involving abuses to the human dignity of the citizenry was inevitable. It was a necessary consequence of the public's perception that local police agencies are incapable of effectively policing themselves. The call by victims, community groups, and review commissions for more federal investigations and prosecutions grows louder and the national exposure being given police brutality and corruption cases by the media grows more intense and compelling. The use of federal authority and the Justice Department to enforce federal judiciary have served as important tools to protect against human indignities suffered at the hands of the police.

The evolution of federal law enforcement to police local law enforcement has served to fill a void created by the public's mistrust and outrage at the continued brutality and corruption exhibited by police across the country. Both the emphasis on constitutional protections against police misconduct and the increased federal involvement in protecting the citizenry from criminal civil rights violations by the police have served the compelling interest in public safety while also instilling some public confidence in our government's ability to "police the police."

REFERENCES

Cole, G.F., Frankowski, S.J. & Gertz, M.G. (1987). *Major criminal justice systems.* Newbury Park, CA: Sage.

Jones v. Marshall, 528 F. 2d. (C.A. 2 1975).

Rowe, P. J., & Whelan, C. J. (Eds.). (1985). *Military intervention in democratic societies.* London: Croom Helm, Ltd.

U.S. Civil Rights Commission. (1981). *Who is guarding the guardians? A report on police practices.* Washington, DC: U.S. Government Printing Office.

Chapter 5

THE ROLE OF THE PRESS IN POLICE REFORM

Marie Simonetti Rosen

With crime going down in almost every major city in the United States, there has been a lot of good news to report about police work lately. But news about the police is rarely, it seems, uniformly good. In one locality after another, news reports continue to tell of police engaging in a virtual laundry list of criminal offenses from stealing hubcaps to child abuse, domestic violence, sexual assault, fraud, bribery, robbery, drug dealing, even murder. One small snapshot, an examination of newspaper stories from around the country during the months of March and April 1997, demonstrates the point: mor than thrity different stories reported incidents of actual or alleged police wrongdoing.

- •10 of those stories reported accusations or findings of excessive force.
- •10 reported allegations of police corruption, much of it drug-related.
- •5 reported police officers being charged with sex crimes.
- •3 reported officers being charged with domestic violence.
- •2 reported officers being charged with drunk driving.
- •1 reported an officer being charged with sexual harassment.

One telling example, in the April 8, 1997 edition of the *Baltimore Sun*, concerned the inability of a federal jury to reach a verdict in the case of a National Institute of Health police sergeant accused of stealing a copy of *People* magazine from the agency's library. (The judge declared a mistrial and the prosecution subsequently decided not to retry the officer.) In what other profession would the alleged theft of a magazine become a news story? Indeed, the likelihood that such a case would even be prosecuted is remote.

But police are held to a higher standard–by the public, by the press, and by themselves. This higher standard evolves from two fundamental facts about policing–officers have the authority to use coercive force, and have been given the responsibility to enforce the law. It is simply unacceptable to society at-large, and incompatible with the rule of law itself, for police to break the laws they are sworn to uphold.

The higher standard for police conduct accounts for why the press pays very close attention to what police do and how well they do it, particularly with respect to allegations of excessive force and corruption, the abuses that cut to the very legitimacy of the police (Ross, 1983). Former police chief Anthony Bouza (1991) noted that it is precisely because police have _more_ power than any other institution in our society that they are exposed to the glare of the media so much and the closer the scrutiny, the greater the magnification of any problems that are found. Police make more than 15.1 million arrests every year in the United States. They have tens of millions of interactions with the public. The vast majority of these interactions go well. A small fraction do not. But police misconduct, at least at the local level, tends to make headlines even when the incident is minor.

There are few institutions of government that are subject to as much oversight as the police: civilian complaint review boards, political officials, local and federal prosecutors, the courts, the Federal Bureau of Investigation, and the Civil Rights Division of the Justice Department in Washington. But beyond them all, the press is a constant watchdog. The press keeps an eye on the police. It also frequently serves as an intermediary between public opinion and police practice. Press coverage, even the anticipation of it, can lead entire departments to change and rethink how they do things. And the attention of the news media can sometimes be more important to the success of criminal justice policy initiatives than legislation (Surette, 1992). Perhaps even more than the general public, the media significantly influences criminal justice officials in developing support for their policies (Surette, 1992).

There is little doubt that the media can shape public opinion about the police. By providing information that readers and viewers use to construct a perception of reality that they then react to (Surette, 1992; Walsh & Mannion, 1993), the media constitute a major force for social change.

Public opinion about the police is generally favorable, though there are pockets of discontent, especially among African-Americans and young people. But all groups are more skeptical when it comes to police using force. The 1995 National Opinion Survey on Crime and Justice, for instance, found that while public opinion was positive regarding such issues as the ability of police to solve and prevent crimes and whether police were fair and friendly, public support dropped to its lowest levels across the board when it came to questions that pertained to the use of force (Huang, Wilson, & Vaughn, 1996).

Opinion polls conducted before and after extensive press coverage of a highly charged use-of-force incident also indicate that public opinion becomes more negative toward the police in the wake of such incidents. For example, a poll conducted in early 1985 by the *New York Daily News* found only 7 percent of white New Yorkers and only 26 percent of African-Americans and Hispanics agreed with the statement that police "often use too much force in making an arrest." But another poll conducted in April of that year, after a highly-publicized case of officers using stun guns to torture a suspect, found that 26 percent of whites and 46 percent of African-Americans and Hispanics now thought police used too much force. Similarly, a Gallup poll conducted for *New York Newsday* in 1988 (in the aftermath of several police-citizen confrontations and accidental shootings) found that 45 percent of New York City residents thought police were too quick to use their guns and used too much force; a year later, Gallup found that only 29 percent of New Yorkers believed that (Flanagan & Vaughn, 1992). Negative press coverage can also increase the volume of complaints against police. In 1986, following the arrest of 12 officers and one sergeant from Brooklyn's 77th Precinct for extorting money and drugs from narcotics dealers, the volume of citizen complaints alleging improper use of force made to the NYPD's Internal Affairs Division began to climb (*Law Enforcement News*, 1987, Jan. 26).

Coverage of police wrongdoing almost always makes news in the area where the event occurred. But, from the press point of view, the intensity of coverage devoted to a story of police malfeasance involves a calculus that takes into account the number of officers involved, their rank, the number of incidents alleged, their nature and severity—is it an isolated episode or has there been a pattern of similar incidents? Other key elements in the equation are how many sources the police reporter has, how forthcoming they are, and what kind of resources can be put into the story. Police scholar Jeffrey Ian Ross has identified several other factors such as the number of media outlets in the area and the status and experience of the police reporters (Ross, 1983). The amount of coverage will depend on what else is going on in the world–wars, elections, important trials, natural and man-made disasters, or major sporting events could all knock the police story on to the back pages. Even the day of the week can influence how much coverage the story will get. Ultimately, all press coverage, including a breaking story on wrongdoing by cops, comes down to time and space. It is an editorial sifting process that goes on in all newsrooms.

Not all acts of excessive force or corruption by police result in a "critical event" (as it is referred to in scholarly circles) or "the Big One" (as some journalists might call it). But there have been stories where the press played an important role in instigating organizational reform of a police agency.

The most notable of these stories began at 12:30 a.m., Pacific Standard Time, on March 3, 1991: the beating of Rodney King by Los Angeles police officers. The beating was witnessed and filmed by George Holliday, who gave his amateur videotape to the media. It was first broadcast locally by KTLA-TV Channel 5, then immediately picked up, nationally and internationally, by CNN. Meanwhile, back in Los Angeles–where, according to Police Chief Daryl F. Gates (1992), the *Daily News* alone ran 500 stories on the King incident in a span of 125 days–a poll conducted by the *Los Angeles Times* found that public opinion had soured on the police department, with 50 percent of residents saying they had lost confidence in the LAPD as a result of the incident (Flanagan & Vaughn, 1992). The continuing media and political fallout led to the appointment of the Independent Commission on the Los Angeles Police Department chaired by lawyer and diplomat Warren Christopher, which found consistent violations of the Department's written policies regarding the use of force, called for the overhaul of LAPD disciplinary procedures, and recommended that police chiefs be subject to 5-year term limits (1991, p.iii, 171-178, 215). After several months of finding himself the focus of the media spotlight, the entrenched, combative Chief Gates announced his retirement.

What made the Rodney King incident different from other episodes of police violence was the way its effects were felt not just locally but nationally. It sent a shock wave through the law enforcement community whose ripples are still being felt nearly seven years later. Departments from Hawaii to Maine began to review their use-of-force policies, and modified or expanded their training programs. Officers were made to watch the videotape of the beating as an example of what <u>not</u> to do. Many localities considered (or reconsidered) the idea of civilian review. Some departments devised computerized systems to keep closer track of complaints against officers. After the events of March 3, 1991, the use of force was scrutinized, both by police and the press, in ways unlike anything seen in more than a decade (Rosen, 1993). Police took a hard internal look at their policies and their practices; the press became more sensitive to the problem of police violence.

Little more than a year later, the Rodney King incident would lead to yet another "critical event." On the afternoon of April 29, 1992, riots broke out in Los Angeles following the acquittal of four LAPD officers who had been put on trial for the beating. The rioting went on to become the worst civil disorder the United States has seen in this century. In south central Los Angeles, some 1,000 fires burned out of control; 52 persons were killed and another 2,383 were injured; more than 16,000 were arrested; and damages were estimated to be as high as $1 billion. And then, in a chain reaction, riots erupted in several other cities. Suddenly, police departments and the press found themselves dealing with issues most of them had not had to face since the late 1960s.

The Rodney King case continues to influence police policy and practice. As a direct result of the incident and its aftermath, a congressional mandate was inserted into the 1994 Crime Act requiring that the U.S. Bureau of Justice Statistics (BJS) collect nationwide data on the use of force by police, with the goal of creating a comprehensive database on the subject. In late 1996, BJS began pretesting questions in conjunction with the National Crime Victimization Survey (which is conducted annually in some 50,000 households). While the information received will reflect the public's experience, similar projects are presently underway that reflect the police view. For instance, a 1994 Virginia Association of Chiefs of Police (VACOP) survey showed that responding agencies made a total of 1,101,877 arrests the year before and used force in only 1,697 (about 0.15%) of those arrests (McEwen, 1996). The International Association of Chiefs of Police is currently at work adapting the VACOP model for a survey of its own.

On the local level, one potentially ominous side effect of the King case has been a growing interest in making the personnel files of police officers available to the public.

• In September 1996, a new law was signed in California allowing reports and other documents pertaining to citizen complaints about police misconduct to be kept in "outer-office" files, where they would be available under state discovery statutes. Police reaction was mixed, especially over the proviso that complaints deemed "frivolous" would not be included. The sponsor of the bill, Assemblyman George House (himself a 30-year veteran with the California Highway Patrol), took the view that officers needed protection from complaints deliberately filed in an attempt to impugn their records by people they have ticketed or arrested. But several California police departments opposed the measure because removing complaints might hinder the efforts of police managers to track problem officers (*Law Enforcement News*, 1996, Nov. 15).

• In July 1996, the Rhode Island Supreme Court stayed a lower court order that would have required the city of Providence to publicly disclose all records pertaining to police brutality and misconduct complaints, including the names of accused officers, even if the complaints were determined to be unfounded. The stay remains in effect until the Court can give the city's appeal a full hearing. Until then, the suit, initially brought by the Rhode Island affiliate of the American Civil Liberties Union, remains pending (*Law Enforcement News*, 1996, Nov. 15).

• In 1995, three Wisconsin newspapers prevailed in a legal challenge against the city of Madison over access to complaints filed by citizens against police. The three papers are currently seeking access to complaints filed against police by fellow officers and other public safety and law enforcement professionals (*Law Enforcement News*, 1997, May 15).

In city after city across the United States, police continue to feel the effects of that 1991 Los Angeles videotape.

In a 1993 study of police violence in New York and Toronto, Jeffrey Ian Ross noted that "police departments... may respond defensively and rigidly and experience internal conflict" in the aftermath of negative media exposure (Ross, 1983). In their 1991 *Controlling Police Wrongdoing*, former Minneapolis Chief Anthony Bouza and coauthor Lawrence Sherman put it this way: "Never is criticism sharper than when it is etched in ink. The hostility toward and suspicion of the press, by such self-protecting institutions as the police, fatefully guide policies in disastrous directions" (Bouza & Sherman, 1991, p. 131). Such was the case with the New York City Police Department in 1986.

Twelve officers and a sergeant assigned to the 77th Precinct in Brooklyn were charged with extorting money and drugs from narcotics dealers. These officers didn't limit themselves to looking the other way; they aggressively engaged in shakedowns. In the face of front-page press coverage of the scandal, then-Police Commissioner Benjamin Ward announced a dramatic proposal to transfer one-fifth of the police force every year. Ward's plan immediately met with denunciation from the Patrolmen's Benevolent Association (PBA) and a city-wide police slowdown ensued. Eventually, a compromise was worked out whereby only new recruits would be subject to the transfers, and would be paired with veteran officers in an effort to extend rookie cops' training while breaking up possibly-corrupting partnerships that might have formed among police academy classmates (*Law Enforcement News*, 1997, May 15). But an unintended, less obvious result of the scandal in the 77th Precinct was the high level of fear of the press that was instilled in the uppermost echelons of the Department. That fear would go on to play a role in the making of another scandal that would occur six years later.

The arrest by Suffolk County police of Officer Michael Dowd and six other members of the NYPD on drug charges made news when it happened on May 7, 1992, but the story did not turn into a "critical event" until five weeks later when the *New York Post* published a series under the headline, "The New Serpico." The *Post* revealed that, beginning in 1988, an NYPD Internal Affairs field investigator, Sgt. Joseph Trimboli, had compiled a case file some 200 pages long detailing drug deals, extortion, and other crimes committed by Dowd and other officers assigned to the 75th Precinct in Brooklyn. But the Department had become so fearful of negative publicity that officials preferred to let corruption continue rather than take decisive action against it, and thereby admit to its existence. Sgt. Trimboli found his investigation repeatedly sidetracked and eventually terminated by ranking members of Internal Affairs in 1990. When Dowd's arrest proved he had been right all along, Trimboli became a whistle-blower; frustrated and fearful of being falsely tarred with the brush of corruption himself, he went to the press with the story of how he had been prevented from doing his job.

The intense media coverage triggered by the Trimboli revelations eventually led to public hearings before a commission headed by former Judge Milton Mollen, which were themselves widely covered in the media and concluded that the New York City Police Department had "completely abandoned its responsibility" to ensure integrity (Commission to Investigate Allegations of Police Corruption, 1994, p. 107).

It does not often happen that an officer will break what has sometimes been called "the blue wall of silence" and go to the press with such damning information about the department or agency to which he or she belongs. But, in New York City, it had happened before. Beginning on April 25, 1970, a series of articles by investigative reporter David Burnham appeared in the *New York Times*. The primary sources for Burnham's stories were two police detectives, Frank Serpico and David Durk. Like Trimboli, they had gone to the press when their superiors would not listen, and when they realized that they were in danger themselves. The *Times* articles pulled back the curtain to reveal systemic corruption within the NYPD. In this case, press coverage of police wrongdoing prompted the appointment of a special commission by the mayor which initiated a three-year investigation of the Department and issued an exhaustive 238-page report that detailed the full extent of police corruption. It led to the resignation of the police commissioner, the appointment of a reformer as his successor, and the creation of a special state prosecutor to probe corruption in the criminal justice system. And it set in place internal procedures to monitor corruption that would themselves, 20 years later, come under scrutiny by the Mollen Commission.

THE POLICE PERSPECTIVE

Many police complain of a double standard in which police are held publicly accountable for their actions while members of the press are not (Walsh & Mannion, 1993). More importantly, they believe that press coverage of police wrongdoing and the use of force has an underlying presumption of police guilt. In defense of the press, Edwin Delattre ascribes its presumption in such cases not to police guilt but to the public's demand that officials always be required to justify their uses of authority or power. "Those who have no stomach for such ordeals of the public trust," he advises, "should choose another line of work" (Delattre, 1996, p. 64).

Police have more contact with reporters than do other members of the criminal justice system. Primarily, police-press interactions occur over crime incidents, and sometimes these interactions have been less than cooperative. Many police feel that the media are relentless sensation seekers. They complain that reporters, especially the broadcast media, interfere at crime scenes and during investigations, and are insensitive to the privacy rights of victims or witnesses (Skolnick & McCoy, 1985). In a 1993 survey of law enforcement personnel, most officers "believed that media personnel are self-serving, profit-motivated individuals with little regard for rights of victims, offenders, witnesses, or the needs of the police" (Walsh & Mannion, 1993, p. 102).

Law enforcement executives and criminal justice scholars alike agree that the media's reporting about police is incomplete, lacking in context and sophistication, and often sensationalized.

Once, most police-journalist relationships were informal, sometimes on the sly, and often involved a drink or two. But in 1966, with the U.S. Supreme Court's decision in *Sheppard v. Maxwell* and the release of the American Bar Association's *Reardon Report*, both dealing with the threat of prejudicial publicity to a fair trial, court officers and police officials began to restrict their communications with the press (Burden, 1981; Kelly, 1991), and the relationship began to become more adversarial. Today, most police departments have full-time personnel whose specialty is public information and press relations, and many departments have written guidelines for dealing with the news media. The International Association of Chiefs of Police (IACP), for example, has promulgated a model policy for the dissemination of police information. It has one brief section that relates to media coverage of possible misconduct by officers, as follows:

> Sensitive information relating to internal investigations of police officers shall not be released without the express permission of the department's chief executive.

A media-relations training session for police "inevitably turns into a forum on the atrocities committed against them or their departments by a hostile and misunderstanding press," in the description of former Chief Anthony Bouza (1991, p. 234). In October 1996, for instance, the IACP's annual conference in Phoenix offered no less than nine panel sessions on dealing with journalists. One was entitled "Media

Brutality." The message was not lost on the local press; the *Arizona Republic* published a story under the headline, "Police Learn to Cover Their Keisters," which depicted the workshops as lessons for police in "upgrading their...ability to evade, equivocate and euphemize."

THE PRESS PERSPECTIVE

Just as police believe the press has too much influence over their operations, journalists believe that police have too much power to set the terms and conditions of their reporting. They complain of a police backlash in retaliation for unflattering news reports, and they are convinced police try to "punish" them by restricting access to information, denying requests for interviews, not returning phone calls, and disregarding their deadlines. Even when official policy dictates an open relationship with the press, hostility on the part of individual police personnel can still interfere with news gathering. A 1988 look at several departments around the country, and at those same cities' major newspapers, found that police departments thought they had a better relationship with local journalists than they actually had (Kobel, 1988).

Reporters also find themselves stymied by dealing with police bureaucracies. Having to submit a written request and wait five business days, as required by the Freedom of Information Act, is obviously no way to gather the news on a timely basis. Reporters therefore need to develop trust with police officials—but getting and maintaining that trust is often difficult. They dislike having to deal with official spokespersons (one longtime spokesman for the Los Angeles Police Department was known among reporters nationwide for having "150 ways to say 'No comment'") and prefer to get information from those closest to the incident. When such sources are not available, they are then forced to seek "secondary" sources—sources, inside or outside the department, who will help get them information quickly that they cannot or will not get from the department's public information unit. Sometimes, as reporter David Burnham noted several years after the Knapp Commission hearings, that means seeking out the malcontents: "These are the people who for varying motives, sometimes good, sometimes bad, sometimes a mixture of both good and bad, provide the reporter with leads, information and documents that the head of the agency usually does not want a reporter to see" (Burnham, 1992, p. 12). But in the hands of an inexperienced reporter, the necessary corroboration may be difficult to get—and the use of such sources may prove risky.

Some police departments are more accessible to the press than others. And some reporters are better than others. The best reporters are the ones who have stayed with the police beat—and they are rare. Echoing many of his colleagues, David Anderson, an assistant editorial page editor for the *New York Times*, has said:

> It is traditional in journalism for beginning reporters to be put on the police beat in order to get their feet wet. Many new reporters want to cover the police only until they prove themselves well enough to move on to other, more glamorous assignments. Police reporting is not considered prestigious, but as scrubby, everyday type of journalism. (Kobel, 1988, p. 13)

It is certainly treated that way at both news outlets and journalism schools. In many newsrooms, the police beat is still assigned to junior reporters who went to a journalism school that, if it offered a course in criminal justice reporting at all, did so only as an elective. This conflict between the low job status of police reporting, and its potential impact, creates an interesting juxtaposition. Policing, as Anthony Bouza and Lawrence Sherman (1991) noted in *Controlling Police Wrongdoing*, remains one of the few professions where the most important decisions are made at the lowest level of the organization. Similarly, the lowest-ranking reporters are sent to cover that organization, with its enormous potential for stories dealing with hot-button issues. Of course, when such a story hits, additional personnel can be redirected by media organizations to cover it. But these reporters are frequently drawn from different beats—and do extra resources necessarily make up for lack of experience in that situation? Since, as Ray Surette, an expert in the police-press relationship, puts it, "The criminal justice system and its component parts are seldom in themselves the subject of news reports" (Surette, 1992, p. 64), the body of knowledge and experience needed to give appropriate breadth and depth to a critical-event story is all too often lacking in the newsroom.

This accounts for why police officials, and criminal justice scholars as well, are frequently exasperated by reporters' lack of basic knowledge about policing, and angered by the distortion of facts and lack of credible corroboration in their stories (Skolnick & McCoy, 1985). And many journalists would agree. Longtime CBS News anchorman Walter Cronkite, speaking at graduation ceremonies for Columbia University's Graduate School of Journalism in May 1997, warned the class that public confidence in the press was in serious decline. Sounding like many police officials, he specifically cited the lack of corroboration in stories based on unnamed sources.

Certainly, whenever an incident occurs involving the use of deadly force, the precursor for many of the deadliest riots in American history, both police and press should exercise caution. The newsworthiness of such an event goes without saying. But the relationship between the police and the press (and the need for both to adhere to the highest standards of their professions) become all the more important at such a moment of crisis, when the stakes are so high.

Currently, several U.S. big-city police departments are undergoing some type of internal change as a result of incidents that involved either the use of force or police corruption, which received heavy local news coverage–Pittsburgh, Wilmington (DE), Charlotte, Chicago, St. Petersburg, and Tucson among them. The elements of reform have many components in common: a change in police chiefs, outside investigations, reports and recommendations, organizational restructuring, policy initiatives and changes in practice, increased training and internal monitors, changes in the recruitment process, and civilian oversight. This is a positive development, since as Jeffrey Ian Ross stressed in his treatise on the politics of police violence, "the police are more amenable...to internal controls than they are to the implementation, in whole or in part, of external controls" (Ross, 1983, p. 78). But internal mechanisms, while they may be more effective, are also more difficult for journalists to cover. What are the reforms? Are they really being implemented? Do they work? For the journalist, the answers to these kinds of questions are to be found in stories that require more skill, acumen, expertise–and interest.

Occasionally, there is a police chief who proves an exception to the rule and who proactively engages the press in order to increase coverage of the department. One such chief was New York City Police Commissioner William Bratton, who in the 1990s took a cue from his predecessor of a century earlier, Theodore Roosevelt. Roosevelt was known to take late-night tours of the city with reporters in tow, seeking to strengthen his hand at pushing through reforms of the police force via newspaper exposures of crime and corruption (Jeffers, 1994). Bratton, entering office just after the Mollen Commission hearings, deliberately turned bad cops into media events. He stripped them of their badges in front of news cameras, "perp-walked" them in front of the press corps, and provided their pictures to the press. Such actions had heretofore been unheard of. But Bratton had a purpose: not only was this new Commissioner using the press to let the public know that the NYPD was serious about reforming itself, he was also using the publicity to send that same message down through the ranks of his own department. During Bratton's tenure, the NYPD took the view that it needed the press in order to reinforce its reforms and strengthen its public image. Indeed, Bratton brought into office with him a Deputy Commissioner for Public Information who had come from the ranks of local television news. The press aide, John Miller, organized reporter "ride-alongs" inside patrol cars and zealously solicited abundant coverage of the Department and the Commissioner.

But the relationship between police and press does not exist in a vacuum. In Bratton's case, his open courtship of the press increasingly vexed Rudolph Giuliani, the mayor who had appointed him. Giuliani personally intervened to force Miller out as Deputy Commissioner, and his ongoing hostility towards Bratton's relationship with the news media was widely recognized as a key factor in the Commissioner's own decision to resign a year later. With the appointment of a much less flamboyant successor, Howard Safir, and what many members of the press corps characterize as Mayor Giuliani's continued enmity, there has been a noticeable decline in reporting about police affairs in New York.

In the wake of "critical event" stories like the beating of Rodney King or the corruption scandals in New York City, the press and the police have learned a few things. Both have become more sophisticated in the way they deal with each other. Reporters have discovered that there is no national barometer of police corruption or improper use of force by officers, and—as more reporters have covered such big stories—the general level of knowledge about police matters in the press corps is higher. Reporting about police issues, while still not to the liking of many in the law enforcement community, is slowly showing more signs of a broader perspective. Consider a 1997 series published in Ft. Lauderdale's *Sun Sentinel* that analyzed the records of 6,630 troubled police officers in Florida. The newspaper found that police misconduct and violence had dramatically increased in the state since 1990 and that fewer officers were being punished for it—a finding that surprised the state's criminal justice officials.

As a result of increasing press coverage of police wrongdoing, many departments are implementing or reinforcing policies and practices that stress respect for human dignity, are changing their traditional recruitment policies, and are establishing more effective internal monitoring systems than ever before. Several departments are participating in a study sponsored by the National Institute of Justice on the use of force, and similar studies are underway to look into the issue of corruption. Police executives know that, at any time, a critical event—a "Big One"—could land on their doorstep, and this realization has led to a process of self-examination. This is a process that has been brought about, at least partly, by the way the news media have covered critical police events. And it is a process that, to many observers of the criminal justice system, has benefited both the public and the police.

Police officers and journalists share a number of similarities in their work—they deal with beats, ask questions, and follow leads; they have to react quickly, exercise discretion, and work odd hours; they are both constitutionally protected in what they do; and they both serve the public. But their mandates are distinctly different. The situation is one that pits the administration of justice against the public's right to know, the right to a fair trial and privacy against the public's right to know, the Sixth Amendment against the First. At its simplest, the police-press standoff is a legitimate, necessary conflict built into our way of life—a conflict of interests between two groups whose missions are both to serve the public good. The public is best served when <u>both</u> camps have well-selected, well-trained personnel who understand the responsibilities of public trust, and who, however grudgingly, respect the role the other plays in a democratic society.

REFERENCES

1987: A retrospective. (1987, January 26). *Law Enforcement News*, p. 3.

Bouza, A. V. (1991). The police and the press. In J.W. Bizzack (Ed.), *Issues in policing: New perspectives*. Lexington, KY: Autumn House.

Bouza, A. V., & Sherman, L. W. (1991). Controlling police wrongdoing. In J.W. Bizzack (Ed.), *Issues in policing: New perspectives*. Lexington, KY: Autumn House.

Burden, P. (1981). The business of crime reporting: Problems and dilemmas. In C. Sumner (Ed.), *Crime, justice and the mass media: Papers presented to the 14th Cropwood Conference 1981.* Cambridge, England: Institute of Criminology.

Burnham, D. (1977). *The role of the media in controlling corruption.* New York: John Jay Press.

Delattre, E. J. (1996). *Character and cops: Ethics in policing* (3rd ed.). Washington, DC: AEI Press.

Flanagan, T. J., & Longmire, D. R. (Eds.). (1996). *Americans view crime and justice: A national public opinion survey.* Thousand Oaks, CA: Sage.

Flanagan, T. J., & Vaughn, M. S. (1992). Public opinion about police abuse of force. In W.A. Geller and H. Toch (Eds.), *And justice for all: Understanding and controlling police abuse of force.* Washington, DC: Police Executive Research Forum.

Gates, D. F. (1992). *Chief: My life in the LAPD.* New York: Bantam Books.

Huang, W. S. Wilson, & Vaughn, M. S. (1996). Support and confidence: Public attitudes toward the police. In T.J. Flanagan & D.R. Longmire (Eds.), *Americans view crime and justice: A national public opinion survey.* Thousand Oaks, CA: Sage.

Jeffers, H. P. (1994). *Commissioner Roosevelt: The story of Theodore Roosevelt and the New York City Police, 1895-1897.* New York: John Wiley & Sons, Inc.

Kelly, P. (1991). The media and the police: Contemporary experiments in cross-education. In J.W. Bizzack (Ed.), *Issues in policing: New perspectives.* Lexington, KY: Autumn House.

Kobel, R. (1988, July 31). The pen vs. the sword: Do police determine the rules and tone of press relations? *Law Enforcement News,* p. 1.

Los Angeles, CA Independent Commission on the Los Angeles Police Department. (1991). *Report* (Summary). Los Angeles, CA.

McEwen, T. (1996). *National data collection on police use of force.* Washington, DC: U.S. Department of Justice, Bureau of Justice Statistics.

New York, NY Commission to Investigate Allegations of Police Corruption. (1994). *Commission report.* New York, NY.

Right to privacy vs. public's right to know. (1997, May 15). *Law Enforcement News,* p. 7.

Rosen, M. S. (1993, January 15/31). 1992 in review: Eruptions, aftershocks and a shifting landscape. *Law Enforcement News,* p. 1.

Ross, J. I. (1983). *The politics and control of police violence in New York City and Toronto.* Unpublished doctoral dissertation, University Microfilms International, Ann Arbor, MI.

Skolnick, J. H., & McCoy, C. (1985). Police accountability and the media. In W. A. Geller (Ed.), *Police leadership in America: Crisis and opportunity.* New York: Praeger.

Some complaints will disappear from California cops' personnel folders. (1996, November 15). *Law Enforcement News,* p. 1.

Surette, R. (1992). *Media, crime and criminal justice: Images and realities.* Belmont, CA: Brooks/Cole.

Walsh, W. F., & Mannion, M. A. (1993). Law enforcement/media relations policy, training and attitudes: A perspective for the 1990's and beyond. *The Justice Journal, 8*(1), 86-107.

Chapter 6

COURSE DEVELOPMENT AND EVOLUTION

JAMES T. CURRAN
MARY D. ROTHLEIN

BACKGROUND

Several years ago, during a one-year period from the fall of 1991 through the summer of 1992, a team of John Jay College faculty and staff developed "Human Dignity and the Police," the course which is the subject of this book. The group working on this project was appointed by John Jay College President, Gerald W. Lynch, and was drawn from a variety of academic disciplines and professional backgrounds. Several members of this original planning team have authored chapters in this book. The product that emerged from the work of this course development team has had a truly profound impact on us, its developers, and, it would appear, on the thousands of police officers who have participated in this learning experience over the past years. The purpose of this chapter is to provide the reader with insight into the thinking of those developing the course, from the inception of their work to the early implementation of the training program.

The process of course development was a slow and somewhat difficult one. The John Jay faculty who were members of the planning group included a philosopher, an anthropologist, a psychologist, a sociologist, and several administrators, including the College's Dean for Planning and Development and Dean for Special Programs. The group's earliest discussions of possible applications of a "Human Dignity and the Police" course focused on local, American, as well as on international possibilities. Discussion of the course's international potential resulted in the emergence of an unforseen problem. One person resigned from the group after its initial meeting, expressing the concern that what we were doing would be used as an imperialistic tool of the American government to force American values and interests on the police of nations other than the United States. The concern that motivated one of our members to abandon the project is not a baseless one. Inherent in the conflict which emerged is an issue of great significance for all educators. This issue involves the role of "values" in the teaching-learning process. We contend that value-free education does not exist and that the teaching-learning process is not a neutral one (Sork, 1988). The mere selection of a topic for a course or program places value on that topic as a result of the decision that it is something important for students to learn. In approaching the design of the Human Dignity course we were clearly cognizant of the ethical issues involved. In no way did we want to force our values on future participants in the course.

NEED FOR THE HUMAN DIGNITY COURSE

Briefly, the rationale for developing the Human Dignity course was rooted in the painful reality that the relationship between police and citizens has always and everywhere been contentious. At best, police-citizen conflict is confined to complaints of cases of rude, insensitive, or unprofessional police behavior. At worst, police-citizen conflict involves brutality, torture, and even homicide. The members of our Human Dignity course development team, because of the specialized mission of John Jay College, spent much of their professional careers studying or working with the police. For this reason, the course development team approached its task with the clear understanding that violation of human dignity was a serious and widespread problem facing police agencies throughout the world.

The charge or mandate given to the Human Dignity course development team was a simple, but a very challenging one. The team was asked to create a course that would encourage police officers to treat the citizens they serve, and to treat each other, in more humane, caring ways. From the earliest stages of its work, the Human Dignity course development team had the advantage of input from the practice field. Three members of the development group had been law enforcement officers. The course was, therefore, from its inception, practically oriented and fundamentally focused on helping the police to accomplish their work in a safe and effective manner, but with an abiding commitment to protect the rights and respect the dignity of all. Fundamental to the John Jay group's discussion of police policies and practices was the belief that imbuing police service with a commitment to sensitive and humane behavior in no way weakens the quality or effectiveness of that service. On the contrary, police who respect the dignity of those whom they serve are more likely to enjoy respect and trust in return. Police agencies that enjoy the respect and trust of the citizens they serve exercise their authority consonant with the collective will of the community.

John Jay College's interest in developing a "Human Dignity and the Police" course was stimulated, in part, by the United States government's response to the widespread movement toward the democratization of governments that continues to occur in many parts of the world, particularly in Latin America and central and eastern Europe. The U.S. government's interest in stabilizing and supporting what were often referred to as newly emerging democracies included not only economic support but a variety of strategies designed to encourage and strengthen democratic institutions. Among these were a number of initiatives designed to facilitate the transition of police agencies from military organizations to civilian controlled and oriented service agencies. One of the ways in which this transition was encouraged was through providing training for police and other law enforcement practitioners.

Initially this training focused on the more technical aspects of police practice, such as investigative techniques, forensic science and technology, and management skills and strategies. It became clear, however, to a number of officials supervising the government's police training effort, that while technical training was of value to police in emerging democracies, it was equally important to provide training for police in the kind of humane, citizen-orientated practices that are consonant with the principles of democratic governance. Our belief that a course which focused on police-citizen relations in democratic states might become part of the United States' training effort in emerging democracies, coupled with our long-standing concern regarding problems in police-citizen relations in our own country, stimulated John Jay College's work on the "Human Dignity and the Police" course.

The Human Dignity course development team was confronted with the daunting challenge of designing a learning experience that would really change the way police would do their job, and the way they perceive themselves, their role, and the citizens they serve. From the beginning, it was felt that if this very ambitious project could be realized, it would be equally beneficial to the police of emerging democratic nations and to U.S. law enforcement agencies where the problems of police-citizen relations are far from resolved.

TRAINING METHODOLOGY

There was never any question that, in order to be successful in achieving behavioral change, the "Human Dignity and the Police" course could not be "business as usual" lecture and discussion training. It was felt that in order to focus the attention of experienced, sometimes cynical, working police officers on sensitive areas of their work, for example, use of force, treatment of persons in custody, interrogation of suspects, we would have to use creative means to "engage" the officers. We knew for certain that any approach which appeared to be "preachy" or didactic would not be effective and might be perceived as condescending.

Instead of viewing our participants as recipients of information, we decided to use an experiential learning approach. We viewed the potential course participants as colleagues and planned to draw upon their experience, knowledge, and analytical ability to infuse the course content. We planned that learning would occur as a result of participation in group exercises and other structured learning experiences.

Experiential training also appeared to us to be the best way to achieve learning goals that include attitudinal change, personal growth, and ethical renewal. Those undertaking such endeavors need to do so in the company of peers and sympathetic guides, sharing ideas and experiences openly without fear of criticism. For officers to have the opportunity to change, we felt that they would need to review and reevaluate every aspect of their work emotionally and intellectually, as perhaps they never have done before. The primary responsibility of the trainer or facilitator in this kind of learning experience is to create and maintain a safe, thoughtful, and supportive learning environment. It was our intention that a student-centered teaching methodology would also help to convey the shared respect for values and viewpoints that is fundamental to the concept of universal human dignity.

To achieve the learning goals that were emerging from our work on the "Human Dignity and the Police" course, we came to realize that it would be necessary to engage course participants in an exploration of the meaning of values and ethics in their own lives. Their memories had to be jarred, and their preconceived notions challenged so that they could examine the attitudes they held about themselves, their families, their colleagues, and the citizens they encounter in their work. Ultimately, the tenets of human dignity would have to become a part of their conscious thinking and their conscious actions (Weinstein & Fantini, 1970). The focal point of those who developed the Human Dignity course, therefore, had to be the students' experience of the course—what would be thought and felt by the participants as a result of what was happening in the course. In discussion, this approach was referred to as student-centered learning and many of the members of our course development team had utilized this approach in other curriculum development projects. It is fair to say, however, that the members of the course development team had never before felt so clearly and so strongly the meaning and import of student-centered learning as they did in their work on the "Human Dignity and the Police" project. The enormity of the task of developing a course that would help police perform their difficult job in a more sensitive and humane way had energized the members of the development team and, in the words of some, resulted in an extraordinarily creative and rewarding work experience.

HUMANISTIC PHILOSOPHICAL BASIS

While it appears that behavioral change can be achieved without attitude adjustment, this approach has limited potential for improving police service since so much of that service depends upon sensitive, humane decision-making in crisis situations. Specific task and role descriptions have limited application because they are void of the intellectual and sensible ability to perceive complex situations, complex individuals, and to assess the implications of whatever decision or decisions an officer has to make on the spot.

Simply said, the most direct way to influence police behavior, to insure that officers "do the right thing," in all of the varied situations they encounter is to somehow foster "right thinking," i.e., to imbue police thought, and thereby police practice, with a fundamental commitment to humanistic philosophy. Indeed, it would be difficult to envision a more appropriate mindset for a police practitioner than a commitment to the philosophy "that holds sacred the dignity and autonomy of human beings" (Elias & Merriam, 1980, p. 109).

"Human Dignity" is a term that was suggested by an experienced law enforcement practitioner/trainer Kris Kriskovich, who, at the time, was in charge of the International Criminal Investigative Training Assistance Program (ICITAP). ICITAP is a United States government agency that provides training and technical assistance for police and other law enforcement organizations throughout the world. Frequently, this work involves assisting police departments and individual officers in making the transition from military organizations to civilian police agencies. Out of this work came the realization that even if the police were extremely knowledgeable about the techniques and procedures of policing, officers could be, in an overall sense, destructive of the spirit of democratic society if they did not have a fundamental commitment to respect the human dignity of each individual, even those who might be considered to be society's outcasts and enemies. Experience also indicated that training labeled "human rights" tended to be viewed by police as rehabilitative at best, and punitive at worst. "Rights" also has the connotation of a structured, tangible, legislated code–an external set of rules which clearly has a purpose but does not provide the inner, ethical consciousness needed if police are to "do the right thing," even when no one is watching. Human dignity, on the other hand, is a broader concept and includes the kind of interpersonal sensitivities, like respect for those in grief, or compassion for the violated, that are impossible to legislate. Human dignity is, however, a concept that is difficult to define, difficult to communicate, and difficult to inject into police training. As educators, we were challenged by the problem of how to communicate this somewhat elusive concept in a manner that would encourage profound understanding and ultimately, implementation in practice.

It was our assumption that, in general, participants in the course would have sufficient knowledge about the unique nature of man in the universe (Overstreet, 1949). Needed, we thought, was an intense, emotional confrontation with the meaning that our shared humanity brought to questions of how we relate to each other. Of particular concern was how the idea that all persons shared a common "human dignity" impacted on the way police viewed their role and viewed the people they encountered in their work.

Humanistic thinking can, of course, be found throughout history and literature. Humanism is central to the works of the ancients, such as Confucius and Aristotle, and was prominent in the philosophical works of the Renaissance. Humanism continued to develop and now is manifest in contemporary thought in various forms, such as existentialism and the self-actualization movement. In 1933, a group of humanists gathered to bring together the primary tenets of humanism and published the *Humanist Manifesto*. It was revised by a larger group in 1973 and published as the *Humanist Manifesto II*. Together with the work of the Association for Humanistic Psychology, these Manifestos set forth the basic tenets of humanistic thought, which include

> An emphasis on such distinctively human qualities as choice, creativity, valuation, and self-realization...An ultimate concern with and valuing of the dignity and worth of man and an interest in the development of the potential inherent in every person. (Misiak, 1973, p. 116)

Our belief in the universality of humanistic values is also supported by the findings of Thomas Cahill (1998) who, after exhaustive research, concludes in his book, *The Gifts of the Jews*, that the tenets contained in the Ten Commandments appear, in one form or another, in all of the major world religions and cultures. Thus, recognition of the unique nature and potential of all human beings and the dignity that all share guided us in our development of the Human Dignity course.

The assumption that humanistic values are universally shared was carefully considered in the light of the diversity of world cultures, religious beliefs, and value systems. Although adopting humanism as a philosophical basis, we were mindful that different societies vary in their tolerance of specific behaviors. For example, the rights and roles of women vary dramatically throughout the world. On such issues as these, it was clear that we had to avoid being judgmental but, at the same time, we had to create a learning environment where the tenets of humanism and the belief that human dignity is innately and equally held by each individual could be understood and accepted, despite cultural variants.

As noted later in this chapter, the Human Dignity course ultimately came to be presented to groups of police officers from dozens of nations and locations. Looking back on the experience of presenting the course for police in many parts of the world—from Central and South America, the Caribbean, Central Europe, eastern European Christian and Muslim countries—provides evidence that our assumption of the universality of humanistic values was a sound one.

Adopting humanism as the basis for the course was further reaffirmed when we offered the course to nonhomogeneous groups. For example, we have had representatives of opposing factions of bloody civil wars in the same course; members of groups that were politically suspicious of and hostile toward each other; and individuals from minority groups that experienced profound, personally traumatic insults at the hands of oppressors. In all of these instances, individual participants were able to affirm their innate human dignity, and acknowledge the innate human dignity of others, including former enemies, victims, and oppressors.

The "Human Dignity and the Police" course that emerged from the work described here has, of this writing, been offered many, many times. The facilitators and participants in the courses that have occurred over the past years can attest to the common humanistic philosophical base that appears to transcend nationality and cultural background.

INPUT FROM PARTICIPANTS: ADULTS MUST ACTIVELY PARTICIPATE IN THEIR OWN LEARNING

One of the most important decisions in connection with the Human Dignity program was made very early in the course design process. For a number of important reasons, several of which were discussed earlier in the chapter, it was decided to involve in a formal way representatives from law enforcement agencies in the course development process. We envisioned soliciting a great deal of input in the earliest stages of course development, including numerous planning sessions, and an experimental pilot offering of the course, with extensive opportunity for practitioner critique built in.

As a result of the basic discussions that initiated work on the "Human Dignity and the Police" course, we at John Jay had a good idea of the learning objectives we would be seeking to achieve. We knew, for example, that we wanted course participants to recognize that violations of human dignity leave permanent scars; that persons in authority can do a great deal of harm in carrying out their responsibilities; that police are a subculture prone to in-group, out-group, we-they attitudes that interfere with objective analysis; that there are reasons why social outcasts are estranged from the larger society; and that, given adequate self-reflection, attitudes and behaviors can change. We did not, however, know enough about day-to-day law enforcement practices and problems in the agencies to be served by the program to develop the exercises, case studies, simulations, and instructor commentaries that would achieve these learning objectives. We needed to place the questions and issues we wanted to address in case studies, exercises, and simulations that were drawn from practical police situations that would seem real to the officers who ultimately would take the course. We knew, for example, that we wanted the students in our Human Dignity course to address the issue of personal responsibility for one's actions. This is a controversial subject in military organizations, like the police, where adherence to the orders of superiors has sometimes been used to initiate and later excuse the most outrageously inhuman and immoral acts. What we did not know, and hoped to learn from our police colleagues, were the kinds of situations they had experienced that would most powerfully illustrate the tension that occurs when an individual's personal sense of right and wrong conflicts with the approach that one's peers or organizational superiors deem "correct."

Another reason why we wanted to work with colleagues in the practice field was our plan to involve them directly in the implementation phase of the program as co-trainers. We felt strongly that if our course was perceived as a collaborative effort of academics and working police officers, we would have the best chance of capturing the attention of the law enforcement professionals who would be taking our course. In summary, we wanted our colleagues in the law enforcement practice field to work with us at every stage in the development of the course. We felt that this was particularly important because the course content, i.e., sensitive interpersonal interaction, along with the student-centered learning approach, were clearly not standard police training practice.

Fortunately, at an early stage in our deliberations, our course attracted the attention of the federal government's ICITAP agency and we were funded to conduct a pilot program that would afford us the opportunity to test our assumptions regarding the design, methodology, and the content of the course. Our agreement with ICITAP provided for a one-week planning session with representatives from law enforcement agencies from twelve Latin American and Caribbean nations. The goal of this planning session was to fine tune our Human Dignity course to serve the specific interests and concerns of police in these participating nations. Included also in our agreement with ICITAP was a plan to conduct an experimental course, if our developmental workshop produced a product that, in the opinion of the participants, and ICITAP, had the potential to achieve its goal of encouraging more humane and sensitive police service. Beyond this, it was anticipated that the course, if successful, would be offered in each of the nations of Central America, South America, and the Caribbean served by ICITAP.

The planning workshop, or pilot project, was successful in that it provided very rich and useful feedback. Armed with this feedback, John Jay's development team revised its Human Dignity course based on the input from our Central American, South American, and Caribbean colleagues. Following this period of revision, an experimental course was ready for implementation. This one-week course was offered in June of 1992 at John Jay College. Participants in the course were selected by their nations' police. The countries represented included Central American, South American, and Caribbean nations. The course was conducted primarily in English, with simultaneous translation for participants, the majority of whom were Spanish speaking. One very important conclusion reached by the John Jay course development team was that its fears about using simultaneous translation to conduct an interactive course, replete with exercises, presentations, role play, etc., were unfounded.

This experimental course, like the first pilot endeavor, was subjected to the rigorous critique of the participants. While the overall reaction to the course was very positive, once again, input from the participants resulted in additional revision. This course was also observed by senior project development personnel from ICITAP and by members of the New York City Police Department's training academy staff. These individuals also provided worthwhile input.

At this point, the John Jay development team felt confident that it had an initial version of its "Human Dignity and the Police" course. It was recognized, too, of course, that in order to respond to new participant populations and changing needs in policing, the course must always remain dynamic—a work in progress.

OVERVIEW OF THE COURSE

The "Human Dignity and the Police" course utilizes a variety of experiential learning techniques, including simulations, case studies, role play, and structured exercises. The concept of human dignity is explored through historical examples and through personal insights provided by the participants themselves. Participants are, for example, urged to recall instances in their lives where they felt their human dignity was violated. They also explore ways in which human dignity can be denied or abused, particularly by authoritarian figures, such as police. A variety of exercises focus on the importance of opening dialog with the community, of implementing a clearly defined code of conduct in police organizations, and of developing training that insures compliance with policies and procedures designed to protect the dignity of both citizens and police. In working groups, course participants develop plans to improve the particular functions for which they are responsible so as to reflect their agencies' commitment to human dignity. In other exercises, participants identify the deviant groups in their societies and develop procedures to better protect the human dignity of members of these "outcast" groups. Participants also plan media campaigns to communicate to the public their agencies' commitment to safeguarding human dignity.

Immediately following its development in 1992, the "Human Dignity and the Police" course was offered under ICITAP sponsorship in over a dozen Central American, South American, and Caribbean countries. The course was enthusiastically received and in a number of countries, both its content and teaching-learning approach were incorporated into police academy training. The "Human Dignity and the Police" course has, in ensuing years, been offered to hundreds of New York City Police cadets, New York City Police officers and New York City correction personnel. More recently, since 1995, the International Law Enforcement Academy in Budapest, sponsored by the U. S. State Department and managed by the FBI, has included the "Human Dignity and the Police" course as a part of its regular eight-week training program for police from Russia and the newly independent states of Central and Eastern Europe. Hundreds of law enforcement officials from the former Soviet Union have participated in John Jay's Human Dignity course at the Budapest Academy. The Federal Law Enforcement Training Center has also included the "Human Dignity and the Police" course in its five-week International Law Enforcement Academy South program which serves police officials from Central American and Caribbean countries. Groups of regional police commanders from Bosnia have taken the "Human Dignity and the Police" course in Vienna, under the auspices of the Austrian government. The John Jay Human Dignity course has also been offered for the hundreds of American police officers serving as United Nations Peacekeeping Monitors in both Bosnia and Haiti. (See Appendix A for complete course outline.) It is noteworthy, too, that ICITAP continues to offer a modified version of the Human Dignity course, originally developed by John Jay College and initially conducted under ICITAP sponsorship. This course is, for example, the cornerstone of ICITAP's training program for police officers in Bosnia-Herzagovina. A third International Law Enforcement Academy has been established in Bangkok Thailand, and once again the Human Dignity course is offered as the first segment of the curriculum.

REFERENCES

Cahill, T. (1998). *The gifts of the Jews: How a tribe of desert nomads changed the way everyone thinks and feels.* New York: Doubleday.
Elias, J. L., & Merriam, S. (1980). *Philosophical foundations of adult education.* Malabar, FL: Robert E. Kreiger.
Misiak, H., & Sexton, V. S. (1973). *Phenomenological, existential and humanistic psychologies: An historical survey.* New York: Grune and Stratton.
Overstreet, H. A. (1949). *The mature mind.* New York: Norton.
Sork, T. J. (1988). Ethical issues in program planning. In R.G. Brockett (Ed.), *Ethical issues in adult education.* New York: Teachers College Press.
Weinstein, G., & Fantini, M. O. (1970). *Toward humanistic education: A curriculum of affect.* New York: Praeger.

Chapter 7

THE EXPERIENTIAL APPROACH:
THE ROLE OF THE TRAINER AND ITS
CRITICAL IMPORTANCE

RAYMOND PITT

Much criticism of police behavior has traditionally come from human rights groups, and police tend to dismiss such criticism as coming from groups they consider to be generally biased and hostile. To change police attitudes, a concept was needed that could help to break through their negative, defensive preconceptions. "Human dignity" was the concept identified by the John Jay College team working on the development of a program to humanize police attitudes. It is a concept central to policing–indeed, to reject it would be to deny fundamental elements of their work, i.e., protection of life and service to people in need. Also, because human dignity is a concept that comes without the taint of perceived ideological antipolice bias, officers can explore its meaning freely, in all its ramifications, without feeling they are being criticized or misunderstood.

THE TRAINING PROGRAM

The "Human Dignity and the Police" training program developed by John Jay College is unique in the way it creates the possibility for police officers to examine, nondefensively, their professional work in relation to the public. Following is a brief description of the course as it is presented in a five-day format.

During the end of the first day, the officers participating in the seminar define what the words "human dignity" mean to them, and select heroes from history who they think exemplify the concept.

By the second day, the participants are recounting their own victimization experiences at the hands of people in authority—both as children, and as members of their own police agencies—as well as the victimization experiences of friends and family at the hands of the police.

On the third day, the group is divided into two subgroups, each bonds as they compete aggressively with the other group of fellow officers. The groups take on all of the characteristics of conflicting parties in society, in-group/out-group attitudes emerge and all of the barriers to communication and cooperation that characterize intergroup hostility can be seen. Upon completion of the exercise, the participants reflect upon their behavior. They then examine how their own police organizations create distance, suspicion, and even contempt for the community, and how their group loyalty leads them to protect bullies and tolerate corruption in their ranks.

By the fourth and fifth days, participants are studying the United Nations Universal Declaration of Human Rights in order to see which Articles most directly apply to policing. Finally, they look at new ways to listen to community needs, to communicate better through the media, and to develop new approaches in training, supervision and management so as to create a new basis for relating to, and collaborating with, the people they have sworn to serve.

This is an incredible amount of ground to cover in any training program, much less in five days. But "Human Dignity and the Police" does so. And what is most encouraging is to see officers openly acknowledging and working on problems that police often deny even exist. "Human Dignity and the Police" has now successfully been offered to police from over forty countries, in a dozen or more different languages.

The Trainer's Perspective

This section describes what the trainers believe makes the program work and how this guides us in our training role.

The key issues from the trainers' standpoint are:
• This is an experiential program.
• The program touches on universally-shared values.
• The program provides an opportunity for self-discovery and self-examination among colleagues. It is honest and challenging and

allows officers participating in it to put aside their defenses and feel free to critically reflect upon themselves in order to arrive at a better understanding of their profession and the formulation of strategies to reform it.

Why An Experiential Program?

There was never any question that to be successful, the "Human Dignity and the Police" program could not be offered in a traditional way. Instead of treating the officers as passive recipients of information from an expert, experiential training treats the participants as colleagues among equals, and uses all aspects of their personalities, academic and professional backgrounds in the training process. Learning occurs as a result of participation in group exercises and experiences that have a dramatic, creative, playful and unpredictable outcome and that require the full engagement of the officer's intellect, emotions, gut feelings, and creativity.

The experiential approach described above is most helpful in training police to become more adept at managing complex interpersonal situations, dealing with suicidal persons or irate citizens or the mentally ill, as well as issues related to gender, racial, or ethnic differences. Experiential training allows officers, in a controlled group setting, to examine their own responses to real-life situations and to hear and watch how their fellow officers respond. Furthermore, through simulations, officers can experience problems from the point of view of the people involved.

Experiential training is also the preferred method when the learning goals are attitudinal change, personal growth, and ethical renewal. Those undertaking such endeavours need to do so in the company of peers and sympathetic guides, sharing ideas and experiences openly, without fear of criticism. For officers to have the opportunity to change, they need to experience every aspect of their work—emotionally, intellectually, and situationally—as they never have before.

The Trainer's Role

The primary responsibility of the trainer in all this is to create and maintain a safe, hospitable, and respectful environment for the police officers in the program, to ensure their full participation. A second, but equally important responsibility is to interfere as little as possible in the self-discovery process while constantly validating what the officers are doing. One of the least helpful things any trainer could do would be to push his or her own agenda.

A third responsibility is to avoid any personal criticism, putdowns, or ridicule that could be construed as violating the human dignity of any of the officers participating in the course or any of the training staff. An overarching responsibility, implicit in all the others, but worth noting directly, is that the trainers serve as a model, as someone whose behavior is directed by respect for dignity; someone who is caring, interested, sympathetic, and supportive of others.

THE PROGRAM EXERCISES

The keys to the "Human Dignity and the Police" course are the exercises and the trainers' and participants' analysis of these exercises.

At the outset, the trainers must establish their credibility with the participating police officers. The trainers present significant biographical information about themselves as professionals, police officers, and/or police trainers. The trainers briefly explain that they have come as colleagues, that this course is unlike any other the participants may have taken, and that the participants are in for a learning adventure they will remember for the rest of their lives.

Since most of the officers have never participated in any kind of experiential program, most come with pad and pencil ready to be given instruction on the nature of human dignity. The participants realize immediately that the course is unique. Perhaps it is the uniqueness of the course–the excitement it generates, the sense of discovery, the participants' involvement through group activity and role playing– that disarm and engage them for the remainder of the program.

Human Dignity: A Working Definition

After introductions, the trainers ask each of the participants to come up with their own word, just one word, to describe what "human dignity" means. Each person's word is important, they are told, and the definition of "human dignity" as it will be used in the course will be the aggregation of all of the words that the members of the group suggest. The officers do this easily but thoughtfully. Going in sequence around the room, they offer typically, words like "pride," "respect," "caring," "duty," "morality," "intelligence," "fairness," and "justice." When finished, there are 50 or so words that stand for human dignity, which are displayed prominently for the remainder of the course.

In early versions of the course, a great deal of time was spent on wordy definitions of human dignity. Many participants labored long and hard at this, and it became clear that limiting the officers to a single word would speed up the process without sacrificing meaning or learning. It would also help the training group as a whole to realize that each officer had his own "take" on what human dignity was, that no one perspective was the "correct" one, and that it was the collection of words, each one complementing the others, that represented the group's thinking.

Human Dignity: Historical Perspective

With a working definition of "human dignity" now established, the members of the group are asked to choose a historical figure whose life championed human dignity. They are asked to "become" that person for a few minutes, and to bring to the group the message they think that figure would want to convey to police officers as we near the end of the 20th century.

Some officers have a hard time "being" the person they have selected. But, sometimes gentle and humorous coaxing from the trainers is required. "Please don't tell me about Gandhi, you are Gandhi and you've come to speak with us."

The officers tend to pick internationally well-known names--Gandhi, Moses, Jesus Christ, Plato, Abraham Lincoln, Martin Luther King Jr., Nelson Mandela, Mother Theresa—as well as heroes of national or local significance. Sometimes their message is a speech, sometimes just a few words. But almost always it is right on target.

"I am Martin Luther King. I believe mankind should live in peace, and that as police we should treat all people in a respectful manner."

Sometimes a collective voice emerges. "I am the voice of the indigenous people who were massacred by invading colonizers over the centuries."

And sometimes it is a voice that could break your heart. "I am Anne Frank. I believe in the goodness of people. And I would ask the police today to make sure that no child ever again has to go through what I went through—that no child will have to chronicle her own persecution."

As the heroic ghosts come forward, one after the other, each a witness to the importance of human dignity as a transcendent issue for our species since the beginning of recorded history, an understanding of the concept clearly takes hold. The initial exercises discussed above have an observable impact on the group. These exercises have required each officer to express a particular word that defines "human dignity" and then to embody a historical figure who has lived, or died for, the belief that each human being is innately endowed with human dignity, and therefore, each is valuable and deserving of respect. And they have done so, while in the company of, before an audience of, fellow police officers.

Human Dignity: Early Negative Experience with Authority Figure

In this exercise, the object is for each officer to express the pain they have felt when their own human dignity was violated by someone in authority whom they trusted when they were young. Trainers ask the participants to share their memory of such an incident with a partner and then to share it with the group.

The officers are not sure how much they dare to reveal, wondering if it would be a mistake to show any vulnerability in front of other officers. That is why the first step—sharing the incident with a partner before sharing it with the entire group—is important. It offers the officers an opportunity to experience personal validation for their story, and to check out its appropriateness before revealing it to the group at-large.

No one is allowed in or out of the training room while this exercise is in progress. The mood is serious and solemn. Officers are asked to listen carefully to each personal revelation. Thus, they appreciate the commonality of the pain of having one's dignity violated.

The stories are often about teachers who falsely accused them of stealing or of cheating on tests, and of being humiliated in front of their class. Sometimes officers recalled sadistic punishment like kneeling for hours on pebbles. Other stories tell of parents, a favorite relative, a trusted neighbor or a coach who erroneously accused them of wrong-doing and refused to believe in their innocence.

During this exercise, it is the job of the trainer to listen—intently, caringly, thoughtfully—and to acknowledge the pain, confusion, shame, ridicule, and the feelings of injustice and betrayal that the officers are remembering and reexperiencing. These traumatic incidents from their childhood, never forgotten, caused a collapse of the respect, admiration, and trust they once had for some authority figure. Typically, they can remember the offending authority's name, exactly when and where the incident happened, and the actual words that were said.

In the violation of personal dignity exercise, the great majority of officers in every class of "Human Dignity and the Police" listen to each other. They sympathize, they empathize, and, perhaps most important of all, they identify with each other, discovering a part of a fellow officer that was not visible to them before. This discovery of their common vulnerable humanity is a breakthrough for the participants in the course. From here on, they know they can trust each other, and the trainers. They truly comprehend the power that people in authority have to humiliate and hurt, as well as to be caring and supportive.

Human Dignity: Negative Experience with Police

At the beginning of this exercise, the officers are randomly separated into four groups of about eight each. The groups have no contact with each other. They are asked to recall incidents when they were civilians in which police officers showed disrespect to them, insulted them, or otherwise violated their human dignity (or that of their family or friends). Furthermore, they are asked to express these incidents through "role-plays," and to literally act out both how the police behaved—and what in their view would have been proper police behavior in the same situation.

What might come as a surprise to law enforcement outsiders is how readily and eagerly officers jump into this part of the exercise. Invariably, they have stories of arrogant officers who openly insulted or berated them when they were younger. Or they can recount vividly how police bullies pulled them or friends and family members over for minor traffic violations, and then used unnecessary force, were verbally abusive, or tried to intimidate and demean them. The participants act out these role-plays with enthusiasm and considerable theatrical skill. As the scenes unfold, the participants watch with mild embarrassment and recognition. Police know exactly how the worst kind of officer behaves. Moreover, they are quite capable of showing the proper way for police to conduct themselves.

After this exercise, stories about police misconduct are no longer an abstraction to these officers. Now they have all viscerally reexperienced and shared what mistreatment by police is actually like when it happens either to them, or to people they know and care about. Discussing these cases of police misbehavior, they are as open and critical as any nonpolice group could be.

Human Dignity: Negative Experience in the Police Organization

Among police trainers there is an expression, "Who will rescue the rescuers?" Police, who are asked to give so much to help others in times of crisis, all too often find no one is there to help when they need help. Part of the reason is that police organizations are quasi-military systems that expect total loyalty from officers–and drill into their personnel the idea that they must accept hardships and difficulties without complaining. This mentality often produces supervisors who show little compassion or understanding.

In this exercise, the officers reenact situations involving violation of their human dignity within their own police organizations. They speak, for example, of being publicly criticized and humiliated in front of fellow officers, of being wrongly accused, of being victimized by a system where who one knows is the only relevant criterion for advantage and advancement. The comments from the group indicate both their shared understanding and their sympathy for one another. They appreciate with greater clarity the power for good or ill possessed by those in authority.

Human Dignity: Group Communication and Achievement Exercise

This exercise is a test of group communication and achievement. On the surface, it appears to be a competitive game, and the officer trainees opt to play it like one. But at its conclusion, the meaning of the "game" comes as a great surprise to the trainees. For some, there is a sense of having been "set up" by the trainers. Others attempt to deny what the exercise has revealed about them. But for most, there is a sobering awareness of the power the group itself has, and the ways in which groups can exercise control over their members while creating distorted negative notions about other or "out" groups.

The game or exercise is conducted in the following manner. The trainers pass out instruction sheets that describe the exercise and are careful not to say much more. The sheets describe the rules of the game. The trainees are to be divided into two groups, blue and green. The groups are physically separated from each other, and are allowed to communicate only through simple message cards. The outcome of these "communications" is detailed in the description of the exercises that follows. A copy of the actual exercise instruction sheet that is given to course participants appears in Appendix A.

The trainers do not in any way interfere with the perception that usually emerges in each group, that the object of the game is simply to win by getting more points than the other group. The teams are asked to keep score and to visually display results as the game progresses. Each group is assigned one trainer who will answer any questions they have. Another trainer serves as the emissary who passes the message cards between the two groups. What the participants do not know is that these trainers are also there to record group process. The trainees are told they have between one and two hours to play the game.

Inevitably, the groups gravitate toward a "war room" mentality. If one team gets a lead over the other, it tries to maintain that lead by preventing the other team from getting any more points. Often a team or group will end the game having acquired only 15 points but sure in their belief that they beat the other team, even though neither has come close to achieving the stated goal of the exercise, i.e., to get the most points possible for their group. Meanwhile, the trainer sitting with the group listens unobtrusively to what is going on, keeping notes on what is being said as the members debate which message card to send.

After the game is over, the teams reassemble. And it is only now, having fully played out the "we win, you lose" behavioral model, that the trainees learn the hidden solution to the game: the way to get the most for your group is to forge a cooperative relationship with the other group. In order to discover this, however, one side (at least) would have had to figure out the game's rationale and initiate a cooperative relationship with the other side.

The trainers make a point of noting how easy it was for people who were previously friendly, and sitting next to each other, to become archrivals, unable to entertain the idea of a cooperative solution—just by randomly separating them into two groups.

During the moments that follow, as the trainers proceed to read aloud from the notes they have taken of the conversations that took place in each of the two groups, a major transition takes place. Although the trainers carefully preserve the anonymity of the officers, as they read back comments, the participants can hear themselves turning hostile, can hear themselves on the attack, can hear themselves supporting the attack. Some hear themselves protesting, but then going along with the group. Mostly they hear themselves talking negatively about the other side. Usually the team that is winning heaps scorn on the losers as "stupid idiots," "weaklings," "incompetents" or worse, while the losing group employs choice euphemisms that indicate they see the winners as "cocky," "sneaky," "insensitive," and "vindictive."

What these officers have just heard unfold is the age-old power of group loyalty at work: the "ins," vs. the "outs," the "haves" vs. the "have-nots," the arrogance and mean-spiritedness of those in power, the seething rage or the passive resignation of the defeated. They have also heard voices of reason and compromise, voices that advocated trying to reach out and move toward solutions that would benefit everyone—and they have heard how, wherever the minority expressed such views, it was silenced by the majority.

At this point the trainer is facing a difficult situation with the group. The "winning" team scored more points, but frequently the members also demonstrated hostility and contempt for their opponents. The losing team sometimes adopts the posture of "righteous victims" and displays the team's own denigrating and contemptuous attitude.

As the debriefing or analytical session unfolds, the trainer's goal is to help the entire group appreciate the ways in which group identity, group loyalty, group behavior (in victory or defeat), and group distrust toward (and dehumanizing of) the "out" group are all part of human nature. We are creatures of group life, and we need groups to survive. At the same time, however, we need respect for human dignity—to protect us from insensitive, hateful, separatist thoughts and the cruel and inhuman behavior that "we/they" thinking encourages. An appreciation for our shared human dignity helps develop collaborative solutions.

This is not an easy task, and it is rarely fully and successfully achieved in the debriefing and discussion following this session. Both formal and informal discussion of this exercise usually continues throughout the remainder of the course. The trainers can, and do, however, make the following points during the formal debriefing immediately following the exercise:

• Group pressures that drown out opposing voices in the heady pursuit of victory are natural, but destructive.

• Those who are not consumed with "leader" or "follower" roles have the ability to think of compromise, mediation, and creative "win-win" solutions. They also have the opportunity, listening to quotes of the team sessions being read back to them, to hear themselves promote or give up on their ideas. They hear themselves succeed or fail to organize support, to assert themselves or sink into passivity, to lead the group toward creative solutions or to follow others, sometimes in the knowledge that others are in error or incompetent.

• The exercise should be viewed as an experiment in a human laboratory wherein participants can review the process and the role they played in it. In doing so, they can better understand how "group process" works, how it can turn the "in"-group against the "out"-group, and how group loyalty sometimes inhibits group and individual learning and initiative.

The Group Communication and Achievement Exercise is, for most course participants, a major learning experience. The participants see how very vulnerable human dignity can be in the face of intense, hostile, "in"-group/"out"-group conflict. There is also a detectable change in the way the participants relate to the trainers after this exercise. They still see the trainers as colleagues, but as colleagues who have helped them to learn a painful, but necessary and valuable lesson.

Human Dignity in Policing: Equal Protection for All, Including Society's Outcasts

The participating officers are divided into four groups. Each group is asked to choose an outcast group in their society—criminals, prisoners, alcoholics, drug abusers, prostitutes, homosexuals, gypsies—who are not only regarded as pariahs but who are also frequently the victims of police abuse. The groups are asked to imagine that they have been assigned to serve on a police board charged with the task of protecting the human dignity of their society's deviant or outcast groups. They are further asked to select one such group and answer the following questions about it:

 • Why are members of group seen as outcasts?
 • How do members of this group view themselves and other people in their society, including the police?
 • What police procedures or training might be necessary in order to better protect the human dignity of this group?

In general, the officers display great empathy and thoughtfulness in this exercise. They are generally sympathetic to the plight of prostitutes, the mentally ill, alcoholics, homosexuals, and even drug abusers. Participating officers are not, however, as sympathetic toward criminals. It appears that police officers tend to see certain outcasts as victims of social conditions, while they see others, like criminals, particularly violent criminals and drug dealers, as having chosen crime and as posing a threat to society. The trainer must be careful not to push an agenda here. It is appropriate, however, to encourage discussion regarding the treatment of those accused of crime, since it is in contact with criminals that many, if not most, cases of police brutality and corruption arise. When certain groups, like kidnappers and rapists, come to be considered not as social outcasts but as being beyond the pale of humane consideration, it makes them far more vulnerable to police abuse.

One approach that has sharpened this exercise is to have each group choose a member to represent the outcast group. The participants are asked to describe to the assembled officers what it is like to be a member of this group and also to critically assess how police actually treat outcasts no matter what the official policy states. This results in very open and spirited discussions.

Professional Ethics in Police Work

The next set of two exercises is designed to help officers explore the ethical issues they face in their work.

In the face of resistance by the participants, it is the trainers' role to ask questions that might help the group address the difficult issues involved. ("Doesn't the police organization, and its attitudes towards 'ratting,' create many of the ethical questions officers face? What about public perception? Can the public trust police if the police won't police themselves?")

The "blue wall of silence," and the accompanying mentality that ostracizes officers who come forward to report crimes committed by police, remains one of the core problems in police work. As the "Human Dignity and the Police" course continues to evolve, the trainers continue to search for approaches that will provide greater illumination and less room for police to evade the issue of police misconduct.

Implementing a Code of Conduct: Making Respect for Human Dignity Live in the Day-to-Day Operation of a Police Agency

In the final exercise of the course, the trainees are told that the Chief of the National Police Agency must make a public announcement within one hour detailing all of the changes that will be implemented in police practice and procedures as a result of the agency's renewed and strengthend commitment to respect the human dignity of all. The participants' task is to present these practical changes to the Chief in a clear and succinct manner so that these can form the basis of a brief public statement by the Chief to the press corps.

The participants are told that "the Chief" will not tolerate any unclear, wishy-washy approaches. He is looking for a tightly-worded program of specific changes.

In the ensuing simulation, the "Chief," usually one of the trainers, acts like a official who really does have to face questioning from the media. He or she is appropriately skeptical and questioning "Is this a real change?" "How can it be carried out?" The result is that our trainees come up with practical and worthwhile ideas, e.g., guidelines on dealing with problem employees, training courses in the police academy that incorporate respect for human dignity, roll-call training that emphasizes the human services aspect of policing, improved performance evaluation approaches that stress respect for human dignity, quality control spot-checking that determines whether the agency's customer friendly policies are carried out in practice, and revised procedures for handling citizens' complaints against officers that assure an unbiased view and fair disposition. The practical orientation of the exercises encourages the participants to understand how they can go about making meaningful changes in the way their organizations relate to the people they are mandated to serve.

Thus the "Human Dignity and the Police" course ends with the participants enjoying a sense of accomplishment and also eager to examine and act on opportunities to create positive change in themselves, their work, and their organizations.

Chapter 8

THE COURSE AS A CHANGE AGENT: IMPACT ON INSTRUCTOR AND IMPACT ON PARTICIPANTS

CARMEN RODRIGUEZ

INTRODUCTION

There is no question that the Human Dignity course has had a tremendous impact on the lives of individuals who have been challenged to participate in five days of introspective, communicative, and experiential learning. There is also little doubt of the profound impact that the course has had on members of the training and development team. Of greatest interest to me, as a member of the team, has been much more the question of why this course effects such change.

In previous chapters, a number of factors have been discussed that can be attributed to the success of the course as a change agent. Among these are an uncompromising set of basic underlying principles that guide both the development and the delivery of the course. These include belief that adults can change both behaviors and attitudes, building excitement into the curriculum through the use of drama and interactive exercises, and the coming together of a team of professionals from diverse backgrounds and experiences in a spirit of true collaboration. These elements combine, like a chemical solution, to create a learning experience that is far superior to the traditional didactic approach, all too familiar in law enforcement training, and to the objectives-driven, bottom-line approach, so prevalent within the training and development field in general. In this chapter, I would like to explore the question of why the Human Dignity course has a powerful effect on the lives of individuals who experience the course either as participants or as trainers. In my estimation, the power of the

Human Dignity course lies in its ability to foster perspective transformation.

I was first introduced to the concepts of transformative learning and perspective transformation while completing a doctoral course of studies at Teachers College, Columbia University. It was during this period that I had the opportunity to study under Jack Mezirow, who at that time served as chairman of the Department of Higher and Adult Education and whose work in critical reflectivity and transformative learning became an important influence in my own work in human resources management and in my personal life as well. Throughout my career in nonprofit, education, and private-sector institutions, my work centered primarily on the behavioristic, objectives-driven, bottom-line approach to learning. Mezirow and his associates offered a new way of thinking about adult development and learning, and a different approach to designing and implementing programs to foster change. Shortly after completing my doctoral work, I was invited to join the team at John Jay College which was developing a new course at the College–"Human Dignity and the Police." At the time, I did not anticipate that my work at John Jay in connection with this course would, in the end, reflect a synthesis of my research interests within the framework of transformative learning.

A BRIEF OVERVIEW OF TRANSFORMATIVE LEARNING

Unlike "instrumental learning," which focuses on learning specific behaviors and tasks, transformative education is most concerned with critically reflecting on one's experience and the premises that have helped to shape those experiences. Mezirow advances the notion that transformative education involves identifying and understanding those early acquired beliefs, attitudes, codes of behavior, habits of interaction, and emotional reactions which in adulthood act as learning boundaries to restrict the acquisition of new knowledge. Through the process of identifying and understanding these learning boundaries, we can free ourselves of unconscious distorted premises and assumptions that get in the way of our further development (Mezirow, 1990).

William Bean Kennedy, professor of practical theology at the Union Theological Seminary and professor of religion and education at

Teachers College, Columbia University and the Jewish Theological Seminary of America, uses the metaphor of a cocoon to describe these learning boundaries. Human beings, he asserts, are formed within the boundaries of limited perspectives. These perspectives begin forming at an early age as a result of our social relationships and our culture—our membership in the family, our circles of friends, and our coworkers in the workplace. Although we may experience a great deal of change in our day-to-day living patterns, these changes take place, for the most part, within the boundaries of limited perspectives.

When we are able to break through our limited way of viewing the world, we experience an opportunity to grow beyond the confines of our "cocoon." By critically reflecting on how and why our social relationships and culture have come to define the way we perceive, we open ourselves to the possibility of expanding beyond these early acquired boundaries, changing our perspectives and acquiring new strategies for interacting with the world around us (Kennedy, 1990).

Perspective transformation, according to Mezirow, can be regarded as the central process in adult education. It is the role of the adult educator to help learners look critically at their beliefs and behaviors, not only as they appear at the moment but at their historical roots and at the potential they have in shaping the future of the learners. The ultimate goal for the adult educator is to create a learning environment where the adult learner understands that he or she can change, if change would provide a more adaptable mindset for contemporary issues and challenges.

The process of transformative learning begins when we experience a "disorienting dilemma," i.e., a situation, often painful, that upsets our inner equilibrium and calls into question our deeply-held personal values and beliefs. These pivotal moments might be triggered by a major change in our personal lives or in our professional lives. A serious illness, the death of a loved one, and divorce or retirement from our profession are some of life's events that may act as the catalyst that begins a process of introspection and leads to questioning of our deepest-held beliefs (Mezirow, 1990).

In the context of educational programs, a facilitator can trigger the process of transformative learning by introducing a problematic situation which leads learners to question the validity of their long-held beliefs, attitudes, and behaviors. In attempting to understand and satisfactorily name the problem, a process of critical self-reflection is required in which learners attempt to identify and critique their assumptions and premises so that they can better understand how and why their individual frames-of-reference have been shaped by their experiences.

Attitudinal and behavioral change does not happen in isolation. Communication plays a critical role in this process since assessing the validity of our beliefs, attitudes, moral and ethical judgment, and behaviors also requires seeing these in connection with other alternative perspectives and experiences. The decision to change our perspective in favor of a new interpretation of our experiences occurs if we are aware of alternatives. Only then, when we can see and assess alternatives, can we make the decision to change or modify our beliefs, attitudes, and behaviors as a result of the newly acquired information. Whether we act upon the insights resulting from this learning process is contingent on whether we have determined the alternatives to provide us with a better way of coping with new situations or whether we have the desire and the will, as well as the resources, to take action in the context of the existing situation.

THE COURSE

The Human Dignity course has proven to be highly effective in setting in motion the process of transformative learning in relation to police work and in fostering change in the lives of course participants. The course was initiated specifically to focus on that dimension of police work that cannot be addressed through technical training. While important and necessary in teaching better ways to perform the technical aspects of the job, "how to" courses do not delve into the connection between the values and moral and ethical beliefs of police officers and the responsibility they have toward those who depend on them for safety and protection. Issues of public fear and distrust resulting from the public's perception, and in some cases observation, of police brutality and corruption move the discussion to a more intense level of inquiry. Thus, the structure of the course brings into sharp relief the contradictions that exist between the ideal role of police in democratic societies and the way individual police officers carry out this role as they seek to protect, to serve, and to preserve domestic tranquility.

Although the training team did not set out to develop a program from the viewpoint of transformation theory, what resulted was a program designed to encourage learners to engage in a process of critical self-reflection with respect to their individual responsibilities as law enforcement officers. By creating conditions within the classroom that allow learners to fully and freely present and examine diverse viewpoints on issues related to police attitudes and behaviors, participants have an opportunity to assess their own preconceived ideas and arguments. This process may lead to a change in the way they view the issues and/or in the way they act upon their beliefs.

The course is structured to move participants developmentally toward a better understanding of how their beliefs and moral judgments help shape the way they carry out their duties as police officers. This is done through a process in which participants (1) confront the painful issues involving police brutality and corruption; (2) frame the issues from the perspective of human dignity by defining this concept, reflecting on it from personal beliefs and experiences, and sharing these experiences and perspectives with their colleagues; (3) operationalize the principles of human dignity through problem solving in relation to real situations; and (4) begin a process of translating the insights and learnings gained in the classroom into a practical plan of action.

The course is structured in a way that requires the learner to probe into the personal values, beliefs, and attitudes that are exhibited when dealing with the public. Through a series of carefully designed experiential activities introduced throughout the course, facilitators provide an opportunity for participants to encounter pivotal moments—disorienting dilemmas—that trigger the process of transformative learning within each individual.

For some, the moment comes during the first exercise in the course when participants are presented with the results of an anonymous survey conducted in the training group. Participants are asked to respond to the survey questions privately, based on their own experiences, and the answers are summarized and discussed in the large group. Participants are then instructed to explore and discuss the answers within small groups. The purpose of the exercise is to begin to name and articulate the very difficult issues that the course seeks to address, and to have participants begin to recognize that their colleagues may, in fact, view these issues from a very different perspective. At a more fundamental level, however, participants may begin to see that contradictions often exist between their private thoughts and personal value systems and the public stance they feel they have to assume. When this occurs in the company of colleagues, individuals see that other police officers face the same conflicts; thus, individual participants begin to understand that they are not isolated in their conflicts and in their desire to do the "right thing."

Professor Raymond Pitt, the Human Dignity program's senior trainer, points out in Chapter 7 how difficult it is to move this exercise from a large group discussion, where the mistreatment of citizens by the police is acknowledged behind a cloak of anonymity, to a small group discussion where participants are asked to reveal whether they personally believe that citizens are mistreated. By using the paradigm of transformative behavior as a basis for explaining behaviors, one sees that the numerous difficulties which inhibit insight and change arise from such things as self-deception, stalling, and backsliding. These behaviors are most common at two points: the beginning of the process when the learner is exposing his/her ideas, values, and sense of order to critical analysis; and the point at which a commitment to take action would logically follow after experiencing an important insight.

At this early point in the course, there are clearly some defense mechanisms operating. Whether we label the behavior self-deception or a fear of how participants feel they might be viewed by their colleagues, this exercise, which merely asks if police practice differs from the ideal concept of police practice, demonstrates the extent to which police officers are trapped within their roles.

While initially frustrating to the training team, the issues survey exercise tested our ability to maintain our faith in the process. A fundamental tenet of transformative education is that although perspective transformation is subject to a number of difficulties along the way, the process itself is irreversible; that is, once our understanding is clarified and we have committed ourselves to integrating this knowledge into our lives, we do not regress before reaching a full understanding and commitment to change. By the end of the first exercise, i.e., the acknowledgment of problems in police work, the training team is satisfied that the issues have been presented in a straightforward way, a dialog has begun, and a safe, hospitable, respectful climate that encourages full examination and exploration of issues has been set for the rest of the course. At this early point in the course, participants have been presented with an initial opportunity to engage in a process of self-inquiry in relation to a number of the major issues confronting police.

The purpose of the next two exercises in the course is to assist participants in bringing the ethereal concept of human dignity to life. These exercises seek to have participants define for themselves what it means when we talk about the human dignity of others, and thereby to establish the frame-of-reference which will guide the rest of the course. The course proceeds with an exercise intended to elicit both individual and group definitions of human dignity. Instead of developing a carefully worded definition, each participant is asked to offer one word that to him/her represents the essence of human dignity. The resulting display of words, on chalk board or newsprint, represents a group consensus regarding what the trainers refer to as a "working definition" of human dignity.

To further explore the concept of human dignity, each participant is asked in the next exercise to reflect on a historical or contemporary figure who embodies the idea of human dignity and who would have something important to say to the police officers gathered for the Human Dignity course. Rather than have participants present these figures in the third person, they are asked to bring them into the classroom, by personifying their champion of human dignity and addressing the group as if they were the champion. In this way, participants step out of their police roles to become messengers of human dignity. This exercise begins to transform the classroom into an environment in which participants can feel comfortable in verbalizing the issues from the perspective of justice, democracy, and moral and ethical behavior without feeling self-conscious in the presence of their colleagues.

Up to this point, the course has been primarily experienced at a philosophical level in which participants reflect on and discuss the universality of the guiding principles of freedom, democracy, justice, equality, moral and ethical behavior, and social cooperation. From the standpoint of transformative learning, the exercises have helped to establish that each individual's frame of reference is shaped by the social and cultural context in which they live. Moreover, the participants begin to understand that the contradictions that exist between what we say we believe and how we actually act when confronted with real world situations test our commitment to these values.

The next series of exercises in the Human Dignity course move the participants from the intellectual level to the emotional realm. These exercises require that participants now shift their perspective to that of a victim. The first exercise in this segment challenges participants to relive the feeling of pain at having their own human dignity violated. This is done by asking the participants to go back in time to when they were no older than 12 or 13 years of age and to recall an incident when an authority figure, whom they trusted, violated their human dignity. They are asked to share the story first with a partner and then with the large group.

The second exercise in this series focuses on the authority of police as exercised upon citizens. It requires that participants reflect on situations in which they or someone close to them—friends or family members—became victims of abuse at the hands of the police, discuss these incidents first in small groups, and present them in the form of role plays to the course assembly as a whole. The final exercise in the series asks participants to reflect on a time when they had their human dignity violated by superior officers within their police organizations. Participants are asked to discuss these incidents first in small groups and thus to dramatically demonstrate through role play the incidents in which they felt a sense of injustice and violation of their dignity.

The objective of this series of exercises is to have participants relive personal experiences of victimization and to recall the feelings associated with those experiences—feelings of humiliation, betrayal, hurt, and vulnerability. In the process, the group is encouraged to arrive at a clearer understanding of human dignity and its meaning in the context of law enforcement and personal interaction. These exercises also result in an increased appreciation for the incredible power that people in authority have to violate human dignity. From the standpoint of transformative learning, participants engage in a process in which they have an opportunity, through critical self-reflection, to recognize the power they have as police and to acknowledge the extent to which they may have individually contributed, in some way, to human dignity violations.

Becoming aware of and acknowledging flaws in our habitual ways of thinking and acting, while difficult, can be tremendously liberating. It can also be psychologically explosive since transformative learning challenges beliefs and values that may be central to one's self-concept. For this reason, the expertise and sensitivity of the trainer are crucial to ensure that in helping learners to reach new insights, the learner's self-esteem is not destroyed and the learner does not become threatened, intimidated, or withdrawn in the process.

To do this, it is crucial that trainers establish a supportive climate in the classroom that allows learners to question, to explore, and to integrate new information into their experiences. The Human Dignity course trainers expend an enormous amount of time and effort to achieve this goal–in both the design stage and during the delivery of the course. It is important for the trainers to find occasions during the course to model the behaviors of respect, interest, listening, caring, and support for self-examination, not only with participants, but among themselves. The team is careful not to push its own agenda, but instead to allow the process to evolve based on the needs of the group at any given point. Trainers are constantly walking the sometimes fine line between valuing and validating the learner's experience. This, of course, requires constant vigilance and ongoing collaboration and discussion among the training staff throughout the duration of the training program.

An incredibly valuable insight that I have come away with as a result of my involvement in this program is that the success of the course hinges on the willingness of the trainers to expose their own habitual ways of thinking and acting to self-scrutiny. Trainers come into the course with beliefs, attitudes, and prejudices that have been shaped by their own limited societal and cultural perspectives. Acknowledging these biases and seeking to understand how and why they have come to be not only helps us to develop and grow as individuals but also as adult educators. In the process of helping others to transform their perspectives, we must be willing to open ourselves to the same process, with all its inherent risks and possibilities. We must be willing to confront those contradictions, if any, that exist between what we believe and what we do in our personal and professional lives. We must challenge ourselves to go beyond any prejudice we may have in order to arrive at a more accurate perspective based on our personal interaction with participants in the course. In this way, the Human Dignity classroom is established as a learning environment where everyone is at once a teacher and a learner.

Ongoing communication among the trainers and between trainers and participants is integral to the course. Because of the central role that communication plays in the process of learning, particularly in the context of transformative learning, the entire third day of the course centers around a communication exercise in which the large group is subdivided into two teams. Each team is given written instructions as to how to participate in an exercise where the goal is to gain as many points as possible for one's team. While the exercise is perceived by participants as a fun game and, in fact, it is fun and interesting, it is also a powerful training tool. Although the stated goal of the game is for the team to earn as many points as possible (nowhere are the teams instructed to "win" the game), team members consistently choose to interpret this goal from a win/lose perspective rather than from a perspective of cooperatively working toward the objective. The group dynamics quickly become competitive and the goal becomes winning at all costs. Frequently, there is one member in the team who recognizes that in order to gain as many points as possible, the strategy has to be one of cooperation. This individual is most often isolated from the group.

There are several insights that are gained from this exercise, including the culture of competition that dominates some societies and the importance of listening to the minority voice in decision-making situations. The power of the exercise as a transformative learning experience, however, is located in an additional element that is introduced by the trainers. A member of the training team is present in each group to take detailed notes on group process. These trainers record, as accurately as possible, every statement made by the participants in the form of direct quotes as the process unfolds. After the groups come together and everyone has had an opportunity to discuss their observations and the insights that they have gained from the process, the trainers take turns reading their notes and providing direct quotes (no one is associated with the statements) which, in many instances, are filled with the kind of scornful verbal attacks that characterize in-group/out-group relationships. Confronted with the fact that an aggressive we/they relationship can be developed between two groups simply by structuring an environment that can be mistakenly interpreted as competitive is an eye-opening experience for course participants. Cautioned to realize how much easier it is for intergroup hostility to emerge when class, racial, or cultural differences separate groups of people, Human Dignity course participants are encouraged to look at the source and validity of any negative attitudes they have regarding persons who are members of groups they identify as "others," "outsiders," or "they."

The remainder of the course challenges the participants to apply these insights into improving police practice. The opening exercises of the course led to a consensus that frequently a disjuncture exists between the value system and perspective of the officer and the way the officer carries out duties. The course also showed how this disjuncture can occur from or be exacerbated by the ethos of the officer's agencies. Now, the ultimate challenge to both trainers and participants is: Can the insight gleaned so far from the course translate into more effective police practice?

The final exercises require the participant to do just that. Perhaps they have to design new recruit training, or to write a mission statement for their police agency, or prepare their commissioner to announce a new policing philosophy and trust. This is the ultimate challenge of the course: Can philosophical, moral, intellectual, emotional reflections be transferred into acting in a more informed, humane way? This is also the challenge of transformative learning: Can reflection result in modification of behavior and practice?

The classroom exercises carried out at these culminating moments of the course strongly suggest success. What is more gratifying are the results set forth in Chapter 12. It appears that the course experience achieves its goals of challenging preconceived notions, of critically reflecting on misassumptions, and finally, seeing participants translate new perspectives and attitudes into behaviors that observably improve the effectiveness of police behavior.

As a trainer, I am in awe of what the police officers who have taken the course plan to do in their practice and indeed do. As a trainer, I am also aware that if I don't evolve in my own profession, in the same way the police participants do in theirs, I have a lost unique opportunity to learn and grow toward a clearer understanding and demonstration of human dignity.

REFERENCES

Kennedy, W. B. (1990). Integrating personal and social ideologies. In J. Mezirow and Associates, *Fostering critical reflection in adulthood: A study guide to transformative and emancipatory learning.* San Francisco: Jossey-Bass.

Mezirow, J. (1990). How critical reflection triggers transformative learning. In J. Mezirow and Associates, *Fostering critical reflection in adulthood: A study guide to transformative and emancipatory learning.* San Francisco: Jossey-Bass.

Chapter 9

HUMAN DIGNITY AND THE POLICE: A PRACTITIONER'S VIEW

ROBERT DONATO

As a professional police officer, the Human Dignity course helped me to focus on the different roles I have in life. Being a cop is just one. I'm also a son, parent, husband, friend, and a human being. A police officer can treat an individual with respect and dignity and still retain his own authority. Treating others with respect does not make one weaker; on the contrary, it makes one stronger.

From childhood, I wanted to be a police officer and to this day, I retain my enthusiasm for my profession. Since I began my career in the New York City Police Department in September of 1980, I have been fortunate to experience and enjoy different assignments. I spent three years as an undercover officer in the Narcotics Division, was subsequently promoted to detective and assigned to the 9th Detective Squad, which encompasses the lower east side of Manhattan. Five years later, I was promoted to sergeant and assigned to the Midtown South Precinct in central Manhattan, which may be the busiest police jurisdiction in the world. While in Midtown South, I was given responsibility for supervising the Community Policing Unit where I began to work, on a very practical level, with many of the issues addressed in the Human Dignity course. More recently, I have had assignments in the Counseling Service Unit and in the Employee Relations Section of the Police Department's Personnel Unit. These last assignments were due in large part to the decision I made in 1992 to enroll in the master's program in forensic psychology at John Jay College. That decision altered my life in many ways.

My studies at John Jay College brought me into contact with a number of faculty and administrators who were working on the development, and later, the implementation of the "Human Dignity and the Police" program. It's a classic example of being in the right place at the right time and, I like to think, with the right qualifications. After learning about the program, I interviewed for and was subsequently selected to become part of the "Human Dignity and the Police" course training team.

At that time, the course was being offered primarily in Latin America. In May of 1993, I was invited to work as a member of a team with the two most senior trainers in the program, Professors Raymond Pitt and Julio Hernandez-Miyares. The course was scheduled to be offered in Peru and after several briefing sessions at John Jay and armed with English and Spanish versions of the Human Dignity course outline I was off to Peru.

Professors Pitt, Hernandez-Miyares, and I landed in Lima. There we were met, in a bullet-resistant Chevy Suburban, by FBI Agent Kris Kriskovich, Director of the ICITAP program under whose auspices "Human Dignity and the Police" was to be taught. After introductions were made, we were informed that, since it was the anniversary of the founding of the Shining Path guerrilla movement, we were to be taken straight to our hotel and were to remain there. Needless to say, the situation made me nervous.

When we were able to leave the hotel, it was to go to the opening ceremony of the seminar. The Attorney General of Peru was in attendance, as was the Deputy Chief of Mission at the U.S. Embassy, Peruvian Army officers ranging from lieutenants up to the rank of major, some prosecutors, defense attorneys, and a judge. Throughout the ceremony, I kept asking myself what I, a cop from New York, was doing there.

After all the dignitaries had departed, we introduced ourselves. There was apprehension on the part of the participants. Clearly, they did not know what to expect from a course entitled "Human Dignity and the Police," which was being given to police officers in the middle of a civil war against a terrorist guerrilla movement in which human rights abuses had occurred on both sides.

One of the first issues raised by the participants was the Rodney King case. It was May of 1993, one year after the L.A. riots and two years after the beating; they had all seen the video. Our response was that policing in the United States was not problem-free, and that issues of corruption and brutality were, unfortunately, universal.

I discovered in Lima, that many of the issues that confront police officers every day are also indeed universal. The Peruvian police officers in our course, for example, had experienced working at a crime scene where numerous civilians were present, but no one wanted to get involved. Such lack of cooperation from the community, they complained, was common. The police commanders frankly discussed how taking money (mordidas) during routine traffic stops was an accepted practice, as was the use of force, both in making arrests and in the interrogation of prisoners (no wonder they solved so many crimes, I thought!).

The Peruvian officers and commanders spoke of many familiar abuses that paralleled abuses in North American criminal justice systems. However, I was surprised to hear that they themselves were often victims of abuse at the hands of their own organizations. They asked me what happened in the NYPD when an officer did something wrong. I explained that depending on the severity of the violation, police officers could be arrested, suspended, have their wages docked, or be punished administratively (loss of vacation, fines, etc.). Peruvian police departments, I learned, could inflict those penalties too; but, in addition, a supervisor could also physically beat a subordinate guilty of wrongdoing.

In my later experiences offering the Human Dignity course for police officers in Bolivia, Colombia, El Salvador, and Panama, I encountered similar histories. Individual officers felt alienated from their communities and mistreated by their own superiors. For most part, the average police officer was poorly trained, minimally educated, and not well compensated. There was an unspoken understanding that the salary could be supplemented with bribes. In country after country, participants spoke of patterns of abuse within their own organizations. One officer told of entering his supervisor's office to find him snorting lines of cocaine. Peer pressure was a common problem; participants reported that informing on a colleague could result in death, or at the very least, the end of a career. In Colombia, participants even told of shootings between police officers, and informed us that an average of 200 officers were killed each year. Also in Colombia, commanders told us that officers who committed even minor infractions were sent to prison for periods up to a month. Some officers who had been given this treatment were in our seminars.

In conversations I had with many of the police officers in our course, they spoke of how, during the course of "Human Dignity and the Police," they had begun to realize just how important the preservation of human dignity is to policing—that it's not simply what they did during their workday, but how they did it that mattered.

I was surprised by the candor of the police officers in our Human Dignity courses—candor which sometimes led to difficult moments. One Colombian colonel told us how members of a drug cartel kidnapped an officer who was the son of a police general and sent him back to his father, in pieces, one body part at a time. "How can you treat criminals like this with dignity?" the participants wanted to know. There is, of course, no easy answer for professional police officers to follow: except to say that when the use of force is necessary, use it, but once someone is restrained and in custody, the use of force should cease, and it is never permissible in an interview or interrogation. On the other hand, when the Human Dignity course was offered in El Salvador, participants who had been members of the FMLN were sitting alongside government police officials. These two groups were opponents in a bitter 12-year civil war that had just ended. By the time our Human Dignity course began, an agreement had been reached. Feelings between the opposing groups still ran deeply, as we learned during the course, and the participants were unusually forthcoming. They spoke openly of how a single event in one's life can have an everlasting effect, about the impact their behavior can have on members of the community, about the role police play at moments of pain and crisis, and how any crime victim who is mistreated by the police has been victimized twice. I was also amazed to hear some of the suggestions for police to build ties to their community. One young Salvadoran detective stated that there should be a television set in every police station, and that youngsters should be invited to visit the station after school so they could watch TV in a safe environment. This service or program would not cost a lot of money, the detective argued, and would allow officers to act as role models for adolescents, ultimately bringing police closer to young people, an important and often difficult to reach segment of the community.

For police to do their job effectively, of course, they need the trust and help of the community they serve. Without the community's cooperation, a difficult job becomes that much more difficult. One way that police/community cooperation can be achieved is by treating everyone with dignity. Police organizations also have to take the lessons of the "Human Dignity" seminar to heart, so to speak, by treating their own members with dignity.

Finally, working with my Latin American police colleagues in the "Human Dignity" program seminars has shown me that the police family is international. It crosses all borders. From the beginning, the police I worked with in Peru, Bolivia, Colombia, El Salvador, and Panama accepted me as one of their own. For my part, I gained a greater appreciation for the talents and struggles of my colleagues in these countries.

Chapter 10

HUMAN DIGNITY AND THE POLICE: A HUMAN RIGHTS COMPONENT OF THE INTERNATIONAL LAW ENFORCEMENT ACADEMY

JAMES PLEDGER

We need not look as far away as Latin America to consider the difficulties of creating a modern, law-abiding police tradition in societies that until recently were dictatorships—or to consider the consequences if the people in newly-freed societies lose faith in democracy, come to equate it with disorder, and yearn for the dictators to return.

All we need to do is look at eastern Europe. Only a few years ago, opposing armies, separated by barbed wire and backed by thermonuclear weapons, faced each other across the heart of Europe. Today, the Cold War is over, and all that is past. Goods and services, ideas and information can now travel across international borders without restriction. But if good things like democracy, free markets, the information revolution, and high technology can travel freely, unfortunately so can organized crime, nuclear smugglers, terrorists, and drug cartels. In the former USSR and the countries of the former Soviet bloc, newly-liberated people are searching for a way to have effective policing without returning to a police state. And we in the West must help them find the way.

Out of this realization came the International Law Enforcement Academy.

The breakup of the Soviet Union and the fall of the Iron Curtain caused profound political, economic, and social changes in those countries. One of those changes was the emergence of crime on a scale previously unimaginable in these societies. Organized crime groups, many with their roots in central and eastern Europe, took advantage of their new-found freedom, and of the newly-established democratic regimes, which did not yet have laws in place to address such sophisticated forms of criminal activity. Indeed, many of the governments themselves became victims of criminal fraud schemes; the privatization of state-owned industries and property, and a banking system in its infancy, proved fertile ground for criminals. With the citizens of these countries expecting economic stability and orderly progress toward a market economy, and their post-Communist economies still in fragile condition, this crime wave had the potential to cause not merely devastating financial losses but disruption and destabilization of the entire transition to democracy.

Meanwhile, throughout the police organizations of the former East bloc, many previous top-ranking managers had been dismissed because of their association with the hated, fallen Communist regimes. In most cases, what remained was a police service with good intentions but inexperienced managers, poorly-trained officers, low morale, inadequate budgets, and few tools to do the job. As the effects of rising crime in the East began to be felt elsewhere in the world, the United States and the West became eager to engage their counterparts across the former Iron Curtain, and to assist the development of these police agencies in learning how to police an open, democratic society.

FBI Director Louis J. Freeh made an official trip through the capitals of western, central and eastern Europe in June 1994, meeting with political leaders and law enforcement executives throughout the continent to begin the dialogue. In these meetings, Director Freeh offered to provide training and operational assistance to the fledgling police services of central and eastern Europe. And he stated his intention to establish a United States-sponsored international law enforcement academy in the region.

With the Director's pledge, the International Law Enforcement Academy (ILEA) was born, with a twofold mission:

• Provide for the personal and professional growth of the trainees, in order to ensure their knowledge of the issues and techniques involved in policing a democratic society.

• Enhance international law enforcement cooperation.

Soon after, personnel from the FBI Academy in Quantico, Virginia and FBI Headquarters in Washington, D.C. surveyed a number of sites for the academy in the former socialist and communist countries.

It was considered desirable, if not essential, to form a partnership with the host government and its police service, and toward that end, the FBI established several criteria, including:

• The host nation's police service must be sufficiently developed, in terms of adherence to the norms and principles of policing a democratic society and also in terms of its operational effectiveness, to be an effective partner with the United States and the FBI.

• The host nation's police service must have sufficient standing with its own government, and its citizens, to facilitate both official and public support for this initiative.

• The city selected as the site of the academy must be easily accessible by air, rail, and automobile, and must be able to support the infrastructure needs of the instructional program.

After reviewing a number of cities, the decision was made to locate the ILEA in Budapest, Hungary, on the existing site of the Hungarian National Police Training and Education Center. The government of Hungary, the Hungarian National Police, and the city itself met all of the FBI criteria. Though constrained by a lack of resources, in just a few years, the head of the Hungarian police, Lieutenant General Sandor Pinter, had assembled a thoroughly-competent executive staff, formed an effective police apparatus, and showed significant progress with his organization. President Clinton and President Goncz of Hungary made the official announcement during President Clinton's state visit to Budapest on December 5, 1994.

A very ambitious schedule was adopted, with the opening of the first course set to coincide with "National Police Day" in Hungary on April 23, 1995–just four months away. To meet that deadline, activity had to proceed on three separate tracks at once:

• Development of a comprehensive curriculum that addressed the crime problems and training needs of each country that would send trainees to the ILEA. The University of Virginia, which has had a long relationship with the FBI Academy, was brought in on the project for its expertise and credibility in this area, and to evaluate proposed instructional programs.

• A "student selection" process that targeted middle managers viewed within their police services as possible future leaders. It was critical that these officers selected for ILEA be well-educated, yet also open to new ideas.

• Securing temporary facilities that would meet the housing needs of faculty and trainees, and the need for "simultaneous translation" in the instructional process itself; also, drawing up plans to renovate the permanent ILEA facility.

Attention then turned to development of the instructional program. To signal that the ILEA was being established so that the U.S. relationship with the participating countries would be one of assistance, not insistence, the curriculum was drawn up via a unique process of consultation and dialogue with the countries themselves. Topics were categorized and ranked in terms of priority, according to the responses expressed by representatives of the member nations' law-enforcement community. It was determined that ILEA training would be oriented not towards new recruits but to mid-career, mid-level police managers. The eight-week sessions would focus not so much on technical police skills as on personnel and financial management; how to conduct and oversee investigations; and how to function as police officers while obeying the rule of law. In addition, the ILEA program would include specialized courses and seminars on topics of particular concern to certain countries.

Several threads ran through the entire curriculum: the need for police in a democratic society to respect human rights; the need for ethics in policing, so that officers would understand their responsibility to serve all citizens fairly and honestly; and the need for strong internal management controls to ensure that police officers are following established policies and procedures. These were sound affirmations of the intent by ILEA's participating nations to complete the transition from authoritarian and totalitarian rule to democratic norms. But with the tight constraints the FBI was facing if it was to begin the first ILEA class on time, a program of instruction in these areas needed to be available immediately; it would take too long to develop such a course *de novo*.

Fortunately, through another wing of the Department of Justice, the International Criminal Investigative Training Assistance Program (ICITAP), it came to the attention of the FBI team working on the International Academy in Budapest that such a human rights-oriented training course for police was already under way in Latin America and the Caribbean. This course, we learned, had been funded by ICITAP, developed by John Jay College of Criminal Justice in New York City, and was used to train (or re-train, as the case might be) police officers in countries that had until recently been ruled by juntas or dictators.

To explore the potential for John Jay's assistance, FBI personnel (including myself) traveled to New York in January 1995 to meet with

Dr. Gerald W. Lynch, president of the College. Dr. Lynch described the course, "Human Dignity and the Police," and it seemed to us like a good fit for the ILEA's needs. With a handshake, we formed a partnership on the spot to work together on Director Freeh's initiative. John Jay College would not only provide instructors to teach "Human Dignity and the Police" at the ILEA, but agreed to participate with the Bureau, the University of Virginia and other federal law enforcement agencies in the ILEA International Curriculum Committee.

"Human Dignity and the Police" is a form of police instruction that has no precedent. Its goal is to provide police officers in developing countries and nascent democracies with a heightened awareness of human dignity as an innate quality possessed by all human beings. Using innovative exercises and learning techniques, its training regimen stresses the importance of the mutually-dependent roles of police and society; the moral and ethical dilemmas inherent in police work; and the impact that peer-group pressure and organizational influences can have on an individual officer's decision-making. In its methods, "Human Dignity and the Police" reflects recent findings in educational research which show that the learner should be an active partner in the learning process, not merely a receiver of information. And, in its objectives, the course is consistent with current trends in law enforcement toward a more humanistic, service-oriented model of policing.

Since our concerns over human rights and ethical police conduct were to be the cornerstones of the entire ILEA program, we decided to devote one full week to "Human Dignity and the Police"–at the very beginning of each eight-week ILEA session. By putting this subject matter up front, there could be no doubt in any trainee's mind, right from the start, about what the focus of ILEA was to be. And, since the course is so interactive in its orientation, involving exercises where officers are required to be full participants and to engage in discussion of various sensitive issues, the front-loading of "Human Dignity" provided us with another practical benefit: it helped "break the ice," enabling trainees to get to know each other and to feel comfortable speaking before the entire class.

The course begins with a discussion of fundamental values that provide the basis for morality, integrity, and professional ethics in police work. In the discussions, participants are asked to identify a word or phrase that best defines "human dignity" for them. They are also asked to cite and portray a historical figure who could be considered a champion of human dignity. Discussion on these two points provides a basis for more in-depth discussion of related issues.

A key element in the course is when all participating officers are asked to examine their personal experiences and discuss a past incident where their own human dignity was violated, especially if the police were involved. These incidents, painful as they are to relate, serve a useful purpose and send a powerful message to the entire class. A group exercise is then conducted that demonstrates the vulnerability of individuals, and society itself, to the power of groups.

Clearly, one goal of "Human Dignity and the Police" is to sensitize participants to the importance of active, two-way communication between the police and the community. All public service organizations, but especially the police, can become self-serving and insulated from the citizens and society they were created to serve. However, the proper kind of police-citizen communication can reduce conflict, generate community support for police activity, and improve police performance. The Human Dignity trainer-instructors also stress the importance of a clearly-defined code of conduct that reflects the value system of the organization and the society. In the latter part of the course, discussions focus on ways to implement such values, not only in a formal code, but in police training, supervision, and monitoring procedures.

On April 3, 1995, "National Police Day" in Budapest, the ILEA officially opened in Budapest. The observance of the day itself was an example of the progress the Hungarian National Police have made under the leadership of General Pinter. In April 1991, the General had organized the first such celebration, featuring displays of police equipment and demonstrations of police tactics, techniques, and strategies. Only a few hundred had attended. By contrast, thousands and thousands of citizens were enthusiastically participating in National Police Day four years later, freely interacting on the streets with the members of their police force—a tribute to the level of trust and respect that had developed in only six years since the end of Communism, and to the work done by the Hungarian police (and General Pinter personally) in reaching out to the people of Hungary. (Indeed, I found myself wondering what the level of public support would be if a law enforcement agency in a major city in the United States were to hold a "Police Day.")

The ILEA, now nearing four years of operation, has educated and graduated approximately 800 officers from some 28 different Soviet-bloc countries in central and eastern Europe, including former republics of the USSR and Russia itself. The reactions from those who have attended and then gone back to their home countries has been very satisfactory. But "Human Dignity and the Police" has been especially well received by our ILEA students. The structure of the course engages the officers, allowing their teacher-trainers to develop genuine rapport with them. And it facilitates their thinking further about the issues involved in policing a free society.

The association between the ILEA and John Jay College continues, with each side seeking out more vehicles for cooperation. This strong link between them has provided a tangible example of the benefits to be gained by partnerships between different levels of government, federal and city, and by the alliance between the law enforcement and academic communities that John Jay has pioneered.

Chapter 11

IMPACT AND IMPORTANCE OF HUMAN DIGNITY TRAINING FOR EMERGING DEMOCRACIES IN THE NEWLY INDEPENDENT NATIONS OF EASTERN AND CENTRAL EUROPE

GERALD W. LYNCH

Budapest was the ultimate test. On January 26, 1995, two FBI agents, James Pledger and Terry Wyllie, visited me in my office at John Jay College. They informed me that Director Louis Freeh was asking the John Jay College to join the Bureau in developing the curriculum for an International Law Enforcement Academy to be located in Budapest, Hungary, where training would be provided for mid-level police officers from the newly-democratic nations of eastern Europe and the former Soviet Union.

Agents Pledger and Wyllie were aware of John Jay's strength in the areas of criminology and criminal justice. They also knew of our course for an associate degree in police science, which we had introduced for recruits in the Puerto Rico Police Academy, and the success we had had there in fashioning a bilingual, cross-cultural program that had been cited for praise by the Middle States Association of Colleges and Universities as "exemplary and worthy of replication worldwide." In addition, Agents Pledger and Wyllie had learned of our involvement with the Justice Department's ICITAP program in developing a new strategy of educating police officer trainees in foreign countries, called "Human Dignity and the Police."

The agents had come to invite John Jay College to join in Director Freeh's initiative to create the ILEA. I was only too happy to agree. A feverish round of meetings followed, first at the FBI Academy in Quantico, and then in Budapest itself.

THE PLANNING MEETING (FEBRUARY 8-10, 1995)

The International Curriculum Committee convened in Budapest to develop the basic format of the ILEA program. The meeting group consisted of representatives of 11 out of the 28 nations whose officers would undergo the training; seven nations that would provide the training; and representatives of the FBI, the Drug Enforcement Administration, the U.S. Treasury Department, the Secret Service, the University of Virginia, and John Jay.

Director Freeh informed us at the outset that he and the Bureau wanted to move with dispatch in launching the ILEA; it was an idea whose time had come, they felt, and diplomatic or logistical delays were unacceptable. The first ILEA class would consist of Hungarians, Czechs, and Poles, approximately a dozen from each country. They would start their training on April 24, less than three months away. Subsequent classes at the ILEA would also include police officers from three different countries: the second class would be from Romania, Latvia, and Hungary; the third from Slovakia, Estonia, and Lithuania; the fourth from Russia, Ukraine, and Bulgaria.

Several sites in eastern Europe had been considered, but its location–as well as the great interest shown by Lieutenant General Sandor Pinter, commander of the Hungarian police, and by the Hungarian government itself–had tipped the balance in Budapest's favor. Major renovations of a former military police barracks on the downtown Buda side of the Danube were being carried out.

The goals in our three days of meetings were to plan a curriculum; select the sequence, duration, and teaching method of issues to be presented in the eight-week course; and determine such things as how to handle simultaneous, four-way translations and the criteria to be used in choosing the officers who would participate. In addition to working with the committee in all these areas, I had an additional goal that was my primary objective in being there: convincing them of the paramount significance and value of the Human Dignity course.

On my first, second, and third mention of "Human Dignity and the Police," there was no supportive reaction from the members. It seemed much easier for those in attendance to talk about money laundering, counterfeiting, nuclear smuggling, the international drug trade and organized crime, and in fact, no less than 54 items were identified as being worthy of inclusion in the ILEA curriculum. Each one of the 54 was then ranked by all the individuals present (with a 7 being the highest rating and 1 the lowest), on behalf of the total of 18 countries represented at the conference as either "participant" or "provider" nations.

In those rankings, "Human Dignity" came in 22nd out of 54—but with a wide variation. The provider nations all gave "Human Dignity" a 6 or 7, as did others such as Russia and Ukraine, whereas most of the participant countries had not seen it as being at all important and gave it only a 1. Nevertheless, I considered this a real victory, since until the votes were counted and the rankings were announced there was no clear way to gauge what the reactions to my arguments had been.

Now the question was: Where should "Human Dignity" be positioned in order to maximize its impact? Some on the committee made the case that toward the end of the eight weeks would be best, since by then the officers would have gotten to know each other well and would be more open to discussing their experiences and feelings. But, based on my experience with the course as we had introduced it in the Caribbean and Latin America, I urged that "Human Dignity and the Police" be given right up front, at the very beginning of the course. This would set the right tone, I said, and signal the officers that their active participation in all phases of ILEA training was encouraged.

It was finally agreed that "Human Dignity" would be given, despite my arguments, in the sixth week of the course. At the end of the three days, Agent Wyllie and I were asked to write the communiqué of the groups activities. With a few modifications, it was unanimously accepted by the group.

BUDAPEST, APRIL 1995: PUTTING THEORY INTO ACTION

The grand opening of the ILEA was set for April 3, "National Police Day" in Hungary. Attorney General Janet Reno and Director Freeh were scheduled to attend the opening ceremonies, but the Oklahoma City bombing, which had occurred days before, forced them to cancel. Instead, the ceremony was keynoted by U.S. Senator Orrin Hatch. General Pinter, of the Hungarian Police, Deputy Chief James Gadsen from the U.S. Mission, and representatives from the Czech Republic and Poland all joined in the official opening, marked by the playing of the national anthems of all four countries involved in launching this new venture.

The course started on Monday morning, and immediately, it ran into trouble. The goal of Day One was to present an overview of the American criminal justice system. By 5 p.m., general rebellion had broken out in each of the three national delegations. Threats to return home were expressed, as was a general discontent with the didactic, day-long lectures, which were described as "confusing," "unnecessary," and "boring."

Led by FBI Agent Pledger, we convened for a late-into-the-night meeting. Near midnight and realizing what we were risking, we from John Jay College, at around midnight, offered to begin the next day by jumping straight into the "Human Dignity" course at 8 a.m. And, Tuesday morning, that is precisely what Dean Jim Curran and Professors Raymond Pitt and Julio Hernandez-Miyares proceeded to do. We were clearly aware that if this failed the blame for the debacle would be squarely on John Jay's shoulders.

The conditions were particularly difficult:

• The room had desks bolted to the floor and fitted out with simultaneous-translation headgear wired to under-the-floor outlets. We had always run the course from around a rectangular table, where all participants could see each other. This conference format encouraged interaction and conveyed the message that our trainer was not a lecturer and the officers were not students who were there merely to listen and take notes. In the classroom at ILEA Budapest, we could not rearrange the furniture to achieve a conference room format; therefore, we would have to adapt ourselves to the already-established lecture-style layout.

• It had already become clear to the FBI that they would not be able to hire translators in Budapest who could translate from all the languages being used to all the other languages spoken by the rest of the officers in the course—not unless the translation went through Hungarian first. Thus, our English introduction of "Human Dignity" would have to go into Hungarian, and from there into Czech or Polish. We were worried about losing a lot in the process. How would our idioms, nuances, and colloquialisms be understood as a translation of a translation?

• Given the history of the Hungarian, Polish, and Czech people, especially in this century, how would such concepts as "human dignity," or the values expressed in the U.N. Declaration of Human Rights, or the ideas of "policing in a democratic society" come across to our audience? Would we be seen as patronizing and out of touch? Would they react to this, as some had to Monday's lectures, as being "totally unnecessary"?

The very first exercise in "Human Dignity and the Police" asks each of the participants to suggest words that characterize their concept of what human dignity is. This simple, cognitive approach usually begins to join the different individuals into a single group as they discuss, argue, and finally agree on a set of words that will provide a working definition of "human dignity" for them. But we had always done this exercise in two languages, Spanish and English. In Budapest, we would have to somehow do this exercise using four separate languages (including English) to communicate with each other. It was a new and unpredictable challenge for us. For instance, Jim Curran explained to the class that one member of each delegation would come up and write, on three different blackboards, the words and phrases suggested by the participants from their country. In English, he said this should be done "in seriatim." But the translation came out that it should be done "simultaneously."

Thus did the first morning resemble the biblical Tower of Babel for us. With Jim, Ray, and Julio trying to explain, and getting nowhere, that each group should go one at a time, a rising (and competing) clamor of Czech, Polish, Hungarian, and English ensued. Our trainers, knowing when they were beaten, retreated to the hallway to consult about what to do. They decided to roll with the punches, go with the flow, and see what happened.

After all the groups had finished writing out their definitions, every word was translated into each of the other three languages. It took time, but it proved to be worth it. The words were amazingly similar, in many cases almost exactly so. As the translated words were heard, bearing such kinship to each other, the groups began nodding and smiling at one another. The process of merging the three delegations into one group had begun.[1]

This episode is symbolic of what is essential about "Human Dignity and the Police." There is no one set way that always works. It is in rising to our challenges, reacting to our surprises, and recovering from our apparent mistakes that we fulfill the course's ultimate purpose: a full and frank examination of how an individual's thoughts and feelings about human dignity can be utilized to make that person a more humane, empathetic, and aware police officer.

That is a tall order, and one that daunts us each time we attempt it. What accounts for our success rate so far? Fundamentally, I believe it is because we practice what we preach: we treat each officer in "Human Dignity and the Police" with dignity and respect, and encourage every officer to speak candidly—about their feelings, their fears, their past traumas, their current problems, and their life's work—in an atmosphere that is totally supportive. We have frequently gotten comments from officers in "Human Dignity and the Police" that this was the first time in their careers when anyone had actually sat and listened to what they had to say at such length. One quoted Mark Twain: "Life is not a dress rehearsal," adding that becoming a police officer had been his choice, but that he appreciated the help the course had offered in sorting out the many dilemmas his job threw at him.

In the meantime, what we see going on in Budapest is a model for the future. Together, we are reaching across national boundaries, and language barriers. We are sharing ideas and information with those who were once strangers to us, and who were (or so we believed) our enemies. We are gaining insights into our different cultures, and our common problems. And we are devising strategies that work, and that all of us can bring back home with us to our respective professional challenges. The results, down the road, will not only be beneficial to participants and instructors but also to our societies. John Jay has been asked to present the "Human Dignity and the Police" course in a new ILEA in Bangkok, Thailand in June 1999. Ten Asian nations will participate including Brunei, Burma, Cambodia, Indonesia, Laos, Malaysia, Paupa New Guinea, Singapore, Thailand, and Vietnam.

---

[1] It should be noted that, while Czech and Polish are Slavic languages with Indo-European roots and are therefore somewhat understandable to each other, and to English, Hungarian is from the Urabic or Finno-Urgic family of languages, and bears no relationship whatever to any other modern tongues except – remotely – to Finnish, Estonian and Lapp. In listening to Hungarian, one strains in vain to hear a Latin, Greek, Germanic or English root word or sound. The suicide rate in Hungary is the highest in Europe, and as a result much has been made of the cultural isolation of Hungary among its Slavic- and Romance-speaking neighbors – not to mention the mystery of the origin of the peoples who arrived on the Carpathian Plain in AD 988, and became the ancestors of

Chapter 12

ISSUES TO BE ADDRESSED IN EVALUATING THE HUMAN DIGNITY TRAINING PROGRAM

BARBARA RAFFEL PRICE

Program evaluation is frequently conducted as part of criminal justice training. In fact, a case can be made that evaluation should be the norm in all training endeavors in order to determine both the effectiveness and relevance of the training.

More specifically, there are several reasons to incorporate a formal evaluation strategy into the criminal justice training process. These reasons include: (1) determining the extent to which the trainees understand the course material presented; (2) determining the extent to which the trainees absorb the course material; (3) determining the extent to which the trainees apply course content after returning to the job; (4) determining the extent to which the application of the course material enhances performance effectiveness, efficiency, and/or furthers the goals of the organization; (5) identification of needed modifications in the training curriculum which might include additional reinforcement training; and (6) demonstrating measurable results as a component of trainer accountability to training sponsors and participating agencies.

In the case of the Human Dignity training, various types of evaluation have been used from the inception. The first time "Human Dignity and the Police" was offered, in June 1992 in New York City, every aspect of the course was an informal evaluation process. Since then, the course has been offered more than fifty times. In addition to United States law enforcement personnel, the course has been offered to police and law enforcement practitioners from dozens of countries in Central America, South America, the Caribbean, central and eastern Europe. The course has been offered on site in many nations, including Hungary, Austria, Colombia, Bolivia, Peru, Honduras, Guatemala, Dominican Republic, Jamaica, El Salvador, Panama, Grenada, Antigua, San Lucia, and Russia.

Three separate evaluation methodologies have been employed over the life of the program. These evaluation methods have included: an interactive survey, an end of course evaluation questionnaire, and follow-up interviews with participants. It should be noted that only the interactive survey was conducted by the course faculty and staff; the other evaluations were conducted by sponsoring agencies, i.e., the International Criminal Investigative Training and Assistance Program (ICITAP) for courses in Central America, South America, and the Caribbean; the University of Virginia for the International Law Enforcement Academy (ILEA), Budapest; the Federal Law Enforcement Training Center (FLETC), for courses at ILEA South; and Dyncorp for training provided for U.S. police serving as peacekeepers in Bosnia. The findings from each of these evaluation methods will be discussed below.

THE INTERACTIVE SURVEY

The first offering of the course was a pilot designed to determine the overall police relevance and acceptability of the notion of human dignity training for the police. Participants included high level officers from the following countries: Bolivia, Colombia, Dominican Republic, Costa Rica, El Salvador, Guatemala, Honduras, Jamaica, Nicaragua, and Panama. The countries clustered into three regions: the Caribbean, Central America, and South America.

The interactive questionnaire contained 25 (Appendix B) questions. Participants were shown a written question on a large TV screen and asked to respond electronically by pressing one of the buttons on a hand-held response device that resembles a TV remote. The aggregate responses of the group were then projected on to a large screen so that a discussion of the group's responses could ensue. For example, one question was "Would it be a good idea to use victims in the training of police?" The group response was: 79 percent, yes and 21 percent, no. The discussion leader then asked the participants to elaborate on these

responses and the implications of such a training endeavor were discussed in relation to the issue of sensitizing police to the morality of
their treatment of citizens.

The topics in this exercise covered personal information about participants, questions related to participants' own experiences of a violation of their personal rights, experiences of having been the targets of
discrimination, police agency information, attitudes about police prejudice, participants' views about crime, views about violations of
human rights at the hands of the police, attitudes about police officer
stress, attitudes about the public's support of police in their home
countries, and about the role of fear as a means of controlling the public. Lastly, the participants were asked about the value of this particular exercise as a way of broaching the topic of human dignity.

Each topic covered by the questionnaire was discussed in the classroom at some length so that participants could express their views and
hear the views of their colleagues. The responses of the group are
found in Appendix B. In order to determine how the police felt about
the need for this training based on their experiences in their home
countries, the question was posed: "Police use of excessive force in
arrests and interrogations is: (1) rare-unusual; (2) frequent enough to
be disturbing; or (3) common." Forty-one percent said "rare-unusual,"
but 59 percent said "frequent enough to be disturbing or common."
Should any justifications for the course and proceeding with additional courses have been needed, this response alone would have
answered that question.

At the end of the exercise, participants were asked their view of the
exercise. One hundred percent said that it was an effective way to get
into the discussion of "Human Dignity and the Police." While this sort
of evaluation tells us little about long-term effectiveness of the training,
it does contribute to process evaluation and would assist in making
mid-course modifications and changes. Following the pilot session of
the course in New York, John Jay's course developers were notified by
ICITAP, the agency that would be sponsoring future sessions of the
course, that electronic processing of the interactive survey would not
be possible in the Central American, South American, and Caribbean
nations, where the course was to be offered. The interactive survey
was therefore reduced in size from 25 questions to 15 and ultimately
to 10 questions. With this reduced number, it could be hand tabulated
quickly so as not to lose the spontaneity that seemed critical to this

evaluation/exercise—what the course trainers indicated that they wanted were unfiltered, uncensored responses. It was felt that this result was best obtained if the questionnaire was administered, tabulated, and critiqued early in the training experience.

Though not quite as rich in information, or as powerful in communicating the need to address human dignity issues, the shortened, hand-tabulated questionnaire proved to have essentially the same impact.

END OF COURSE EVALUATION QUESTIONNAIRE

A second form of evaluation was administered to subsequent courses. The evaluation questionnaire was administered by ICITAP staff at the conclusion of each of the more than approximately twenty courses offered under ICITAP sponsorship.

This evaluation questionnaire is relatively simple and brief. It consists of twelve Lickert Scale questions and three open-ended questions. The results from one course are representative and will serve to illustrate the findings produced by this method of evaluation.

The results are based on the responses of 27 out of 30 officers—sergeants and inspectors—from the Jamaica Police who completed the evaluation form following their attendance at the week-long course. Responses were overwhelmingly positive on the Lickert Scale questions through which the participants rated couse content and trainees' capabilities.

The three open-ended questions asked: "Would you please tell us what was most valuable about the course? What was least valuable about the course?" and "Do you have any suggestions for changes or improvements in the course?"

The answers to the first question from the Jamaica Police centered on the fact that as a result of the course, many participants were made aware for the first time of the importance of their behavior as it relates to the dignity of other people. They also reported that they had a new appreciation of the critical nature of human dignity and of the fact that police can make a positive difference. On the question of what was least valuable about the course, they observed unanimously that the entire course was valuable. On the question of suggestions which would improve the course, some said the course was too short, some said no changes are needed, several suggested videotaping the course so that police trainers could replicate parts of the course in order to expose other officers to the course content. Several participants recommended that management level police officers should also be exposed to the course. None of the comments were negative; rather, all comments expressed a positive, constructive tone and content. As a device for immediate feedback from participants on their views concerning the value of the course, the questionnaire appears to be quite effective. Hundreds of responses to this questionnaire from participants in Human Dignity courses conducted throughout Central America, South America, and the Caribbean were very similar in nature to those of the Jamaica Police, as reported above.

In 1994, when the Human Dignity course began to be offered under U.S. State Department sponsorship at the International Law Enforcement Academy (ILEA) in Budapest, Hungary, a somewhat different evaluation form was introduced, also a Likert-type scale. This form is administered by ILEA staff immediately following completion of the Human Dignity portion of ILEA's eight-week training curriculum. Evaluations have been excellent throughout 16 training sessions as the results of ILEA Budapest sessions (Appendix C) indicate.

FOLLOW-UP INTERVIEWS

In 1993, ICITAP and John Jay College sent a survey evaluation team to Honduras and Jamaica to study the implementation of the human dignity skills and concepts covered in the training. This evaluation occurred six months after the course was given in Honduras and four months after it was held in Jamaica (see Appendix D). The team, including Drs. Julio Hernandez-Miyares and Raymond Pitt, interviewed 38 of the 55 participants who had attended the two courses. It was the view of the team that the course had a greater impact on police officers in both countries than had been expected. In Honduras, where debate continues on the question of civilianization of the police and the role of the military, efforts have begun to institutionalize Human Dignity training by incorporating it into the police academy curriculum. In Jamaica, Human Dignity training was incorporated into the academy curriculum. Another positive outcome was that participants were aware of human dignity in their personal lives, i.e., improvements in their interpersonal relations with family, colleagues, and the citizens they were serving. In both countries many participants told the team during the interview that the course was extremely important in their lives and that it had made a deep impression. Some reported that they continue to struggle with the significance of the course in their lives.

The interviews further revealed that in Honduras the course has prompted changes in the internal disciplinary machinery within the department. Now guidelines have been developed as to when disciplinary measures will be taken and officers are given explanations of disciplinary sanctions rather than just receiving punishment. The training has fostered increased debate on the use of force as a police function. In the treatment of prisoners, the interviews revealed that the officers have greater understanding of the psychological implications of rights violations; the use of abusive language in dealing with detainees has also been prohibited.

Lastly, the interviews indicated that as a result of the training, the Honduran police have greater clarity of their role as public servants and better understand that treating the public with respect does not mean relinquishing police authority.

In Jamaica, according to the interviews conducted after the training, participation in the Human Dignity training led to a wide variety of institutional and personal changes. Interviewees reported improvements in both their personal lives and within the police agency. They indicated that their lives were made easier as a result of the course because the skills they acquired enabled them to use new interpersonal strategies both at work and at home. For example, they reported that at home their ability to communicate with their families improved and that they were less rigid in their dealings with their children.

With their police colleagues, they reported that the course increased their understanding of problems faced by women colleagues, increased their intervention with police who abused subordinates and heightened awareness of police abuse. The course also led to new insights concerning criticisms from the community about police behavior with the result that they now do not take complaints "as something personal" against the officer who is criticized.

In the treatment of prisoners, the course has led to more appropriate handling of mentally ill detainees, prompter medical attention for detainees, greater sensitivity to the possibility that a person might be wrongfully detained, and improvement in the sanitary conditions of the jails.

Thus, the results of the interviews with participants led to the conclusion that those who participated in the Human Dignity course reported extensive behavior changes and great satisfaction with the benefits accrued to them by attending.

Lastly, according to the interviews, police interactions with the community have improved in terms of greater sensitivity to victims of crime, tourists' complaints, the handling of domestic disputes, dealing with young groups, and ghetto residents. Interviewees report less complaints about police abuse, a general effort by the police to have community complaints about the police addressed, and better treatment of Rastifarians.

In conclusion, it is fair to say that the evaluations of the Human Dignity course over many years, and with diverse national populations, have shown a high degree of success of the program. The course has not only benefitted individual participants but has had an impact on police agency policy and police practice. What cannot be measured is the positive effect the course has had on citizens who have come in contact with the police who have reported such positive results.

The developers of the "Human Dignity and the Police" still maintain the desire to evaluate the impact of the course on participants after intervals of two to three years. Unfortunately, funding to date has not been available for such follow-up studies.

Chapter 13

THE FUTURE: WHAT WILL IT BRING?
WHAT WE MUST DO?

GERALD W. LYNCH

Police officers often describe the complexities and danger inherent in their work by offering something like the following definition of police work: A police officer must meet each person with respect, with a willingness to help, with professional objectivity–and must have a plan to kill him.

No discussion of human dignity in policing can ignore the dangers involved in police work. We require police officers to accept risks to their safety in a way that is asked of few others in our society.

In order to protect our lives and property, and to protect themselves as they do so, police officers carry guns. This makes their profession unlike any other civilian one, and delegates to them a unique and enormous power over other people. And, unless they are properly socialized and trained to understand the limits they must impose on themselves, and the compelling reasons behind those limits, they are apt to misuse that power.

As hazardous as their job is, the dangers in police work do not excuse misconduct by police officers. Unfortunately, examples of police misconduct are all too commonplace in America today. The Rodney King case, for example, shocked the world, as television screens around the world carried the videotaped spectacle of Los Angeles police officers apparently far exceeding the use of necessary force in subduing a prone suspect who did not appear to be actively resisting. In the summer of 1997, New York City and the nation were disgusted by the revelation that, at a time when members of the NYPD were a part of a United Nations peacekeeping mission in Haiti, seeking to retrain that nation's police after generations of dictatorship and terror, a Haitian immigrant was allegedly beaten and then brutally abused inside a precinct station house by New York City police.

The purpose of the "Human Dignity and the Police" course is to make (or, if need be, turn) police officers into professional, humane, service-oriented guardians of the peace. Despite our success with the course in so many parts of the world and despite the gratification we at John Jay feel over the uniformly high ratings "Human Dignity and the Police" has received from the officers who have participated in the course, we do not believe that even replicating this course in every police department will remake policing into the professional model it needs to become.

For that to occur, much more fundamental change will have to take place in the recruitment, training, and education of police officers. Police must join every other profession by being educated, in a university setting. Then (again, like every other profession), after their university education, police should undergo their preservice training in firearms, departmental rules and regulations, defensive tactics, and all other job-specific training. But the essential preparation for police officers must take place in colleges and universities across America.

Western civilization has developed a unique system of higher learning that prepares the next generation for the responsibilities of leadership while also training them in the practicalities of pursuing a job or a professional calling. From their medieval origins in Bologna, Paris and Oxford, universities have led the way in teaching and research and, working closely with the professions, have brought about much material progress, too.

Here in the United States today, we may have been outclassed in steel, cars, televisions, and cameras, but no nation comes close to us in the quality, breadth, and diversity of our 3,800 institutions of higher learning which students from all over the world stream into this nation to attend. Yet in the beginning, American higher education had as its specific purpose merely to educate men (exclusively) in the fields of divinity, medicine, and the law. A great leap forward came with the Morrill Act, the so-called Land Grant Act of 1862, when farmers teamed up with major universities to create the marvel of modern American agriculture. Later, when the dry goods salesman, the banker, and the auto dealer joined forces with higher education, they created the great business schools. Likewise, the builder, the mason, and the carpenter combined with the power of the academic community to create leading schools of architecture and engineering. In the 20th century, we have seen the disciplines of education, social work, and nursing become full partners in degree-granting, liberal-arts education within the university. Even the military has recognized this necessity and joined the trend; the various branches of the service today all have their distinguished academies, not to mention the Army and Navy War Colleges for postgraduate, mid-career training of future top leaders.

Law enforcement remains one of the last major professional callings in America that relies on insular, nondegree-granting academies that have little or no affiliation with higher education. Police education has stayed not only separate, but narrowly focused. There is no liberal arts curriculum in police academies, nor does the curriculum routinely discuss much historical, philosophical, moral, and public-policy issues of the day related to police work.

It would save cities and states across America millions of dollars every year if, like every other profession, police officers received their education, their job training, and their badge—in that order. And how should police be educated? I believe the answer is simple and unequivocal: like everybody else. Separate, insulated police academies are not only not equal to their collegiate colleagues, maintaining this system is actually what prevents policing from becoming a true profession.

The still-prevalent model of the police as separate and distinct from the rest of society in the way they are trained and educated can be traced back to the assumptions of Sir Robert Peel, who founded the "Police of the Metropolis" in London in 1829. Sir Robert, whose officers came to be nicknamed "Bobbie" after him, basically sought to hire night watchmen who could sound the hue and cry for help if miscreants were at work. It was their brawn and alertness that was of value, not much more. They were not supposed to be gentlemen; therefore, they needed no education.

Contrast this with the approach of J. Edgar Hoover almost a hundred years later. Upon taking over the Federal Bureau of Investigation, Hoover required that his agents not only graduate from college but also either be lawyers or certified public accountants. Whatever else may be said of Mr. Hoover and what occurred during his five-decade reign as director, he was dead right in demanding that his agents be fully and rigorously educated before they could even begin their FBI training.

Unfortunately, the model chosen by Sir Robert Peel is still much more the norm than the standard set by Hoover and the FBI; the failure of policing to fulfill its potential as a profession is precisely because higher education is not required as a prerequisite.

In the 1960s, President Lyndon Johnson made a great contribution to American policing by championing the Law Enforcement Education Program (LEEP), which provided the funds for more than 500,000 police officers to begin their college education. Today, former LEEP students constitute the largest part of the cadre of more than 150,000 American police officers who have attained baccalaureate degrees. Although the LEEP Program was terminated more than twenty years ago, its impact continues to be felt. Moreover, law enforcement agencies are raising their educational standards for admission to the police service for promotion, to supervisory and management positions.

How, then, will these new standards affect the future behavior of American police? What impact will they have on historically-entrenched patterns and practices of corruption, brutality, misuse of force, and other abuses of authority?

I believe we can envisage the day when the mentality of professional policing will replace rote obedience to the "blue wall of silence," and when a professional standard of conduct and integrity will be a more powerful motivation for police officers than will the negative subculture of any particular department. This will never come about, however, if police agencies simply add more in-house courses targeted to emerging local problems, nor will mandating more well-intentioned but ineffective "community relations" sessions for newly-promoted officers.

If that course of action worked, it surely would have done so by now. Nothing short of a wide-ranging, liberal arts education for every police officer has any chance of breaking the lock that local departments and their "culture" have on each succeeding generation of new recruits.

When the vast majority of the police "profession" perform in accordance with a code of conduct and ethics such as the United Nations Universal Code of Ethics for Law Enforcement, or many of the codes developed by individual police agencies and organizations, there will be a standard to supersede the "customs," mores, or accumulated bad habits of any particular jurisdiction. A reporter from the San Juan *Star* in Puerto Rico follows the same journalistic code as a reporter from the San José *Mercury-News* in California. A psychologist from Portland, Oregon follows the same guidelines of ethical behavior for the practice of therapy as does a psychologist in Portland, Maine.

Are there violations of ethical codes, committed regularly, by members of any profession that has such codes? Certainly there are. But they are clearly seen as such. Violations of a profession's code of ethics are viewed as a fundamental betrayal of what the profession stands for. Those who are guilty of such betrayals are punished and ostracized from that profession for their transgressions.

The ultimate test of a profession's validity and credibility is whether it can police itself, and the criteria for passing that self-policing test are:
• whether the profession's standards are acceptable to the public;
• whether those standards are the norm for conduct locally;
• whether, via the process of peer review, meaningful penalties—warnings, censure, and dismissal—occur on a regular basis, without favoritism or bias.

None of these criteria can be met, and thus the test cannot be passed, without a national and, indeed, international core of similarly-educated police officers who, in the course of their educational experience, have grappled with the moral and ethical issues involved in policing.

To take one example of the inability of American law enforcement to police itself, we have the record of the largest and perhaps the premier force in urban America, the New York City Police Department. With regularity, every 20 to 25 years for the last century, an independent civic commission has had to be set up to deal with police corruption scandals in New York: 1894, the Lexow Commission; 1913, the Curran Commission; 1932, the Seabury Commission; 1949, the Dewey Commission; 1970, the Knapp Commission; 1993, the Mollen Commission.

After every scandal, there has been a wave of reform—for a time. Theodore Roosevelt became Police Commissioner after the revelations of the Lexow Commission and swept the New York City Police clean of corruption. Patrick Murphy arrived in 1970, in the wake of the Knapp Commission and revelations by Detectives Frank Serpico and David Durk that massive bribe-taking had infested the Police Department. Murphy proceeded to institute the most far-reaching, innovative reforms since Roosevelt's time.

The Commission to Investigate Allegations of Police Corruption (the Mollen Commission), frustrated by the collapse of the Department's anticorruption mechanisms, formally proposed a permanent, independent body to engage in external oversight of the police. The final report called for a "two-track strategy for improving police corruption controls."

> The first track...focuses on strengthening the Department's anti-corruption apparatus with equal emphasis on improving the quality of recruits, enhancing police training, strengthening supervision, upgrading methods of prevention, strengthening internal investigations, enforcing command accountability and attacking the root causes and conditions that spawn corrupt acts.
>
> The second track urges the creation of a permanent external police commission, independent of the Department, to:
>
> (i.)Perform continuous assessment and audits of the Department's system for preventing, detecting and investigating corruption;
>
> (ii.) Assist the Department in implementing programs and policies to eliminate the values and attitudes that nurture corruption;
>
> (iii.) Insure a successful system of command accountability;
>
> (iv.) Conduct, when necessary, its own corruption investigations to examine the state of police corruption.
>
> The Police Commission would make recommendations for improving the Department's integration and will deliver reports of its findings and recommendations to the Mayor and Police Commissioner for appropriate action. In essence, the Police Commission would serve as a management tool for the Mayor and the Police Commissioner and a watchdog for the public. It would identify problems of police corruption and corruption control that need immediate attention, and insure that the Department will not again fall victim to the pressures that work to corrupt its anti-corruption systems. (1994, p. 152)

The "first track" proposed in the Commission's final report was supported by all interested parties, including the Police Department itself. The "second track," a permanent, outside investigative body, won the support of the New York City Council, the *New York Times*, former Mayors David Dinkins and Ed Koch, and many others, including myself, but not that of Mayor Rudolph Giuliani or then-Police Commissioner William Bratton or now - Police Commissioner Howard Satir

When the Mollen Commission issued its report, some observers wondered if the failure to heed and implement its recommendations would sow the seeds for another police scandal. A spate of brutality charges in the late 1990s suggests that perhaps these concerns are well-founded.

There should be two fundamental, and overriding, goals in the profession of policing. The first is to police the community. The second is to police the police. Unless the second goal is pursued with as much intensity and commitment as the first, the police will inevitably find that their ability to meet that first goal has been fatally undermined.

The demand to identify and remove corrupt or brutal officers must come from the men and women who are out on the street every day and night, doing the job of policing in America. There is, however, little chance this will ever come about unless and until there are universally-recognized professional standards for police officers, with real and immediate sanctions for violations of those standards. In turn, there is little chance that will ever come about unless and until there is universal higher education required of every officer, prior to admission to the profession of policing.

As "Human Dignity and the Police" has helped show us, we live in a world that is becoming more diverse, more complex, and in some ways, more dangerous. In times like these, the education and training of police officers takes on more importance than it ever has before. In the work of police in the 21st century, it will not be so much the caliber of the officer's weapon that matters in a crisis, it will be the caliber of the mind and heart of the officer.

REFERENCES

New York, NY Commission to Investigate Allegations of Police Corruption. (1994). *Commission report*. New York, NY.

APPENDICES

Appendix A

HUMAN DIGNITY AND THE POLICE: MORALITY, INTEGRITY AND PROFESSIONAL ETHICS IN POLICE WORK*

---

* Course Development and Presentation by John Jay College of Criminal Justice, The City University of New York

Part 1: Outline for Trainees

COURSE NARRATIVE

Values are first learned in the context of our earliest and most intimate relationships—our families and closest friends. It is in such relationships that we learn empathy and caring, honor, respect, integrity and fairness. Long before we began our professional careers, we learned these fundamental values, and we have had many opportunities to make critical decisions involving truth, justice, and human dignity. The challenge of this course is, therefore, not to impart new values but rather to reacquaint us with our existing values and to affirm their centrality in our lives and in our day-to-day work.

The goal of the course is to imbue police practice with a sharpened understanding of human dignity as an innate quality possessed by all human beings. Further, the course encourages examination of morality, personal integrity, and professional ethics.

The course provides an opportunity to reflect on our experiences and to assess behavior in terms of whether it is consonant with, or conflicts with, our deeper sense of right or wrong. We know, for example, that sometimes peer pressure can, and does, support negative or destructive behavior. We also know that it is difficult to change behavior when it is strongly reinforced by group or organizational mores.

We will look at what we do, why we do it, and the role that values and professional ethics play in our lives and in our work. We will seek to sharpen our understanding of human dignity and examine the unique power of police to protect or assault the dignity of those whom they serve.

This course is not taught in a traditional way. It is designed to achieve experiential learning by using nontraditional teaching and learning methods. The course will be most meaningful if both trainers and participants approach it as an opportunity to work together on important issues of common concern.

COURSE GOALS AND OBJECTIVES

• Initiate discussion of the meaning of human dignity and its importance in police work.

• Provide a historical perspective for the study of human dignity in contemporary police work.

• Facilitate vivid recall of incidents in which participants experienced violation or denial of their human dignity.

• Encourage participants to appreciate fully the importance of human dignity, the pain of its denial and the power and impact of authority figures, particularly the police.

• Explore the impact of peer group and organizational influences on individual behavior.

• Examine the influence of peer pressure on police practices in relation to social deviants and outcasts.

• Confront the moral questions facing police.

• Examine issues of personal integrity and professional ethics in police work.

• Establish the fundamental role of personal responsibility and individual decision-making in determining behavior.

• Reinforce the importance of a police agency having clearly defined codes of conduct that reflect the formal value system of the organization and the society.

• Identify ways in which the goals and values stated in a code of conduct can be implemented on a practical level by a police organization.

• Identify training, supervision, monitoring, and sanctioning strategies to assure compliance with police agency policies and procedures that protect the dignity of both citizens and police.

MAJOR TOPIC OUTLINE

• COURSE ORIENTATION
• THE MEANING OF HUMAN DIGNITY IN OUR LIVES AND IN OUR WORK: DEVELOPING A WORKING DEFINITION OF HUMAN DIGNITY
• HISTORY OF HUMAN DIGNITY
• PAST PERSONAL EXPERIENCES WHERE HUMAN DIGNITY WAS VIOLATED
• EXAMINATION OF VIOLATIONS OF HUMAN DIGNITY IN POLICE-CITIZEN CONTACTS AND IN CONTACTS AMONG POLICE IN POLICE ORGANIZATIONS

• GROUP IDENTIFICATION AND THE POWER OF PEER GROUPS: LAW ENFORCEMENT AND MINORITY GROUPS
• PROFESSIONAL ETHICS AND POLICE WORK: CASE STUDIES IN ETHICAL DECISION MAKING
• POLICE CODES OF CONDUCT: A WORKSHOP IN PRACTICAL APPLICATION OF THE UNITED NATIONS CODE OF CONDUCT FOR LAW ENFORCEMENT OFFICERS

DESCRIPTION OF INSTRUCTIONAL MODULES

Course Orientation

Activities at the outset of the course will include introductions, discussion of the purpose of the course, the style in which it will be taught, and its potential impact on participants and police organizations.

The Meaning of Human Dignity in Our Lives and in Our Work: Developing a Working Definition of Human Dignity

The innate nature of human dignity and its essence or fundamental qualities will be explored.

History of Human Dignity

Human dignity will be examined as an ideal to work toward—a goal never fully achieved, but nevertheless vitally important in the continued quest to maximize human potential. A brief historical review will establish that the quest for human dignity is not unique to any era or any part of the world.

Past Personal Experiences Where Human Dignity Was Violated

Confrontation with the painful reality of past encounters in which dignity was violated will stimulate understanding of the capacity of authority figures to have a negative impact on the lives of others.

Examination of Violations of Human Dignity in Police-Citizen Contacts and in Contact among Police in Police Organizations

Participants will be asked to recall an experience in which, as civilians, their dignity was violated by police. Participants will also be asked to recall and discuss ways in which they, as police officers, have been disrespected, abused, or dehumanized by their own police organizations. Participants will work in subgroups to identify the most frequent or most devastating violations. Role play simulations will vividly demonstrate violations and how they might be prevented.

Group Identification and the Power of Peer Groups: Law Enforcement and Minority Groups

A structured group decision-making exercise will simulate peer support and peer pressure in relation to group expectations and the achievement of group goals. Participants will also be asked to identify outcast groups and address the issue of providing protection and police services to societies' pariahs.

Professional Ethics and Police Work: Case Studies in Ethical Decision-Making

Brutality and corruption, no matter how widespread, or how strongly supported by peers, ultimately result from personal decisions of individual police officers. Strengthening the personal code of ethics of each police officer is therefore the most direct and fundamental step that can be taken to eliminate police abuse of authority.

This session explores how individuals process information and act on it. Behavior is examined as the product of multiple influences, past experiences, peer pressures, etc., but ultimately determined by the individual's personal perception of what is good and evil, just and unjust, right and wrong.

Police Codes of Conduct: A Workshop in Practical Application of the United Nations Code of Conduct for Law Enforcement Officers

The widespread existence of Police Codes of Conduct demonstrates that there is broad general agreement that respect for human dignity is a fundamental principle of proper police practice. Yet despite an apparent consensus on what should be done, violations are commonplace and indeed call into question the practical impact on some agencies of their formal commitment to a code of conduct.

Course participants will be asked to augment the United Nations Code of Conduct for Police and to apply ethical principles in determining the appropriateness of police practice. Participants will also be encouraged to recognize that by personal commitment and example they can influence the extent to which respect for human dignity is reflected in their personal lives and in the policies and practices of their agencies.

Part 2: Manual for Instructors

ORIENTATION

Objectives

- Introduce participants, trainers, agency and other officials present.
- Introduce purpose of the course.
- Establish climate of participation, open discourse, candor, and engagement.

Instructional Approaches

- There should be a brief general description of what the participants will experience in the course. It is particularly important to stress the fact that the course is not conducted in the traditional lecture/discussion manner. Participant involvement is vital and responsibility for learning and teaching is shared by all trainers and participants. The enterprise might best be described as professional colleagues joining together to address an issue of mutual and fundamental importance.

- Trainers should introduce themselves providing background information that clearly establishes their credentials to facilitate the Human Dignity course (while maintaining their modesty, of course).

- Course participants should be introduced and greeted. Introduction of course participants can be by the participants themselves. This is an opportunity to learn what participants are expecting from the course and to initiate their involvement and participation.

DEVELOPING A WORKING DEFINITION OF HUMAN DIGNITY

Objectives

• Stimulate and organize the group's effort to define human dignity.
• Encourage broad analytical thinking regarding the essence of human dignity.
• Participants should emerge from the exercise comfortable that they, both individually and as a group, have defined human dignity with sufficient precision to move on to look at the concept in their work and in their lives.

Instructional Approaches

Although the manifest goal of this session is achievement of a working definition of human dignity, the discussion whereby this is achieved is equally important. It is anticipated that the definition that emerges from this process will be an important artifact–a "word-picture"–ideally on a large chalkboard or on flip charts that remind participants of the words they have used to define human dignity. In a way, this exercise permits us to reconfigure the training space into a kind of "chapel" of human dignity (with words that define human dignity physically present in the environment of the group) and to continue the rest of the course in that chapel.

Participant Activities

Participants will be asked to select the word or phrase that best defines human dignity for them. Discussion will contribute to the group's working definition of human dignity that will serve as a reference guide throughout the course.

HISTORY OF HUMAN DIGNITY

Objectives

• At the conclusion of this exercise participants should have a clear "intellectual" grasp of human dignity and should recognize that the quest to achieve human dignity is an ongoing one–probably as old as our species.
• The discussion of the history of human dignity and the exercise which asks participants to invite a historical figure to join in that discussion, should

reinforce and make more vivid the groups' working definitions of human dignity and thereby build on and reinforce previous learning.

• Human dignity will be examined as an ideal to work toward–a goal never fully achieved, but nevertheless vitally important in the continued quest to maximize human potential. A brief historical review will establish that the quest for human dignity is not unique to any era or any part of the world.

Instructional Approaches

In this exercise it is important to achieve and retain focus. We are inviting, as if by divine or demonic intervention, a visitor from beyond. This visitor will, we speculate, have something important to say to police officers in the final years of the 20th century. Keeping this focus is vital. Potential detours are many and seductive (i.e., "let me demonstrate how much history I know"). The trainer's role is to get as much human dignity content and insight into the groups' discussion as is possible by linking discussion of human dignity to memorable persons or events throughout history and thereby establishing human dignity as a vital concern throughout the ages.

Participant Activities

Participants will be asked to select and portray a figure from history who was a champion of human dignity and to imagine what this historical figure would say to us as we embark on this course.

PAST PERSONAL EXPERIENCES WHERE DIGNITY WAS VIOLATED

Objectives

• This exercise can be a powerful encounter with the pain of having one's dignity violated.

• Participants learn that dignity violations can leave permanent scars and that those in authority can do a great deal of harm, as well as a great deal of good in carrying out their responsibilities.

Instructional Approaches

Flight from the pain and feelings of vulnerability that this powerful learning experience engenders is understandable and generally occurs in the following ways. Participants will, for example, say:

• "Recovery from being "hurt" makes you stronger"–suggesting that there is a good outcome to dignity violations.

• "There is great dignity in forgiving the abuser"–and the greater the abuse the more dignity in the forgiveness of the forgiver.

• "Discipline is important in life even if it hurts–look at what permissive parents and schools have done to our children."

Analysis of the violations described in response to this exercise will help the group to avoid being detoured by the "escape routes" mentioned above. For example:

• The violations of dignity mentioned are often profound–and occur under circumstances where the individual violated is most vulnerable and there is high risk of life-long trauma–not really the stuff for psychological muscle toning.

• Forgiving the violator is perhaps linked in some way to personal recovery from traumatic experiences, but it is not particularly useful in confronting the enormous potential that those in authority have to damage the dignity of those whom they encounter in their work.

• The violations described are not generally the result of discipline or a demanding environment per se, but rather the result of treatment that the participants characterize as clearly unfair, terribly cruel, horribly embarrassing, etc.

Participants leave this portion of the course, aware of what it feels like to have one's dignity violated and the enormous potential that authority figures have to violate human dignity. In summarizing the experience, trainers may choose to emphasize the tremendous potential that authorities have to do good, or evil, to help or hurt someone when they are most needy or vulnerable.

Participant Activities

In groups of two, participants will relate to each other an early experience in which human dignity was violated by an authority figure, e.g., teacher, relative, older, more powerful peer. Participants report to the group at-large and discuss the impact of their experiences.

EXAMINATION OF VIOLATIONS OF HUMAN DIGNITY IN POLICE-CITIZEN CONTACTS AND IN CONTACT AMONG POLICE IN POLICE AGENCIES

Objectives and Instructional Approaches as in previous section.

Participant Activities

• Participants will be asked to recall an experience in which their dignity or the dignity of someone whom they know very well was violated by the police. Participants will work in subgroups to identify the most frequent or most devastating violations. Role play simulations will vividly demonstrate the violations and how they might be prevented.

• Participants will be asked to recall and discuss ways in which they, or police agents or officers whom they know, have been disrespected, abused, or dehumanized by the police organization. Participants will work in subgroups to identify the most frequent or most devastating violations. Role play simulations will vividly demonstrate the violations and how they might be prevented.

GROUP IDENTIFICATION AND THE POWER GROUPS: LAW ENFORCEMENT AND MINORITY GROUPS

Objectives

• To demonstrate how in-group/out-group-we/they attitudes are produced and experienced by participants in a group communication exercise.

• To illustrate that participants' behavior in subgroups exhibits a broad range of the in-group/out-group conflict that separates people in a society.

Instructional Approaches

• Trainers can encourage the participants to look at their experiences in the subgroups and to reflect on how similar group affiliations and experiences can separate groups of people from each other in our communities.

• The trainer's role is to help participants to recognize what group membership means—the good (identity, encouragement, unqualified love and support) and the bad (loss of objectivity re: outsiders, uncritical conformity attitudes, and behavior driven by need for peer approval).

• In discussing the outcome of the exercise with participants, it is important to stress the fact that competition is a natural reaction to the experience and indeed a competitive approach is not "wrong" in and of itself. The point to be made is in situations where people are interdependent, cooperation is often the key to achievement since the alternative—the success of some at the expense of others—is not a just or stable social condition.

Participant Activities

• Participants will engage in a group exercise that simulates experiences of group commitment, group loyalty, peer group pressure, and group achievement.

• Participants will be asked to work in subgroups assigned to develop specific strategies that will protect the human dignity of social deviants and outcasts in encounters with the police.

PROFESSIONAL ETHICS AND POLICE WORK: CASES IN ETHICAL DECISION-MAKING

Objectives

• Establish the fundamental role of personal responsibility and individual decision-making in determining behavior.

• Confront the moral questions facing police.

• Examine issues of personal integrity and professional ethics in police work.

Instructional Approaches

These exercises examine behavior as the product of multiple influences, but ultimately resulting from a personal cognitive decision for which the individual is responsible. It may take a great deal of persistent encouragement from the trainers to surface the idea that behavior is a complex product influenced by experience but ultimately determined by the individual cognitive process. In this area, more than in any other area of the course, creative trainer intervention is necessary if issues involving personal responsibility for one's actions are to be confronted sensitively and candidly.

Participant Activities

• Participants will be asked to assess the behavior and motivation of a fictional member of the police service, a young person early in his police career who, since entering police work, has become involved in a situation where his truthful statements resulted in criminal charges being filed against fellow officers. The young officer, now ostracized and the victim of personal threats, is depressed and discouraged about his future in the police service.

• Participants working in groups will be asked to determine the ethical course of action in a variety of common police situations. Groups will also be asked to recommend strategies that prevent unethical behavior and/or encourage professional, ethical practice. After group discussion, presentations will describe ethical solutions and strategies to insure ethical practice.

• Participants will be asked to reflect on their careers in the police service and to describe the most difficult ethical decision they have had to make in their professional lives.

POLICE ETHICAL CONDUCT CODES: A WORKSHOP IN PRACTICAL APPLICATION

Objectives

• Reinforce the importance of a police agency having clearly defined codes of conduct that reflect the formal value system of the organization and the society.

• Identify ways in which the goals and values stated in a code of conduct can be implemented on a practical level by a police organization.

• Identify training, supervision, monitoring, and sanctioning strategies to assure compliance with police agency policies and procedures that protect the dignity of both citizens and police.

• Assess what has been learned in the course and how it can be applied.

Instructional Approaches

• This session reinforces, through practical application, the importance of recognizing the human dignity of all persons in carrying out the responsibilities of the police service. Trying to make a professional ethical code of conduct live in the actual day-to-day practices of a police agency is a confrontation with reality and commitment—an acid test of resolve.

• In facilitating the code implementation exercise, it is effective to simulate the pace and tension of a high-level staff meeting, prior to an important press conference. The trainer or participant portraying the police executive who is being "briefed" can do a great deal to help the training group make its transition back to the workplace by asking very tough practical questions. Trainers can probe in order to determine if learning in the course appears to be leading toward tangible impact on personal behavior and/or agency policy and practice.

• At the conclusion of this session, participants should be able to assess whether the course is of practical value in their day-to-day work. Trainers can help to achieve this learning goal by encouraging candid confrontation with real issues throughout the exercise.

Participant Activities

Participants will divide into four groups. Each group will be asked to assume that it is responsible for one of four major functional areas—training, first-level supervision, area or regional management, and response to citizen complaints. Each group will be asked to develop a plan on how respect for human dignity and professional ethical practice can be strengthened and reinforced in their respective area of responsibility. Groups will be asked to present their findings to their agencies' chief executive officer who is about to meet with the press to discuss a major initiative to provide even more effective, responsive, and professional police service.

Part 3: Exercises

HUMAN DIGNITY: A WORKING DEFINITION

Take a moment to think about human dignity. Use. the space below to write several single words that best describe what the term human dignity means to you, e.g., *Respect.* Please be prepared to share your thoughts with the group so that we can have a common understanding of human dignity that will enable us to discuss the concept meaningfully in our course.

_____

_____

_____

_____

_____

_____

_____

_____

_____

_____

HUMAN DIGNITY: HISTORICAL PERSPECTIVE

The quest for human dignity is as long as the history of the human species. Take a few minutes to select one or more champions of human dignity (may include recent or present day history makers as well as persons from the past) whom you think would make a valuable contribution to our discussion in this course. Be creative in your choice. Consider social reformers, philosophers, governmental leaders, philanthropists, representatives of oppressed people, etc. Use the space below, if necessary, to write the person's name and the message regarding human dignity that he or she might bring to us if they could join us today.

Imagine then that you are this historical figure and prepare to say what you think he or she would say to the police officials in this course on human dignity if he or she (the historical figure) could join us today.

Please meet with your group to discuss the historical figures and their messages and select approximately six for presentation to the course assembly as a whole.

HUMAN DIGNITY: EARLY NEGATIVE EXPERIENCE WITH AUTHORITY FIGURE

Please reflect on your childhood and pre-adolescent years (school years) and identify a painful experience with someone in authority (parent, older relative, teacher, athletic coach, trusted friend, etc.) who insulted you or hurt your feelings–an experience that you now realize violated your human dignity.

Now turn to the person next to you, with whom you are paired for this exercise, and tell your partner about the experience and the impact it had on you. Then, be prepared to share the experience with the group as a whole.

HUMAN DIGNITY: NEGATIVE EXPERIENCE WITH POLICE

Please describe to your partner for this exercise the most negative encounter or experience–insult, disrespect, violation of dignity, mental or physical abuse–that you or someone whom you know very well (family or close friend) have experienced in an encounter with police.

Now, meet with the other members of the group on NEGATIVE ENCOUNTERS WITH POLICE and:

• Discuss your negative experience with the police and the negative experiences of the others in the group.

• Identify three or four incidents or situations that exemplify the most common, most frequent, and most destructive negative encounter or experiences that people have with the police. These situations may be drawn directly from specific personal experiences discussed in the group or based more generally on the group's discussion of negative encounters with the police.

• Work with your group to develop ways to present to our entire assembly of course participants the three or four experiences or encounters your group has identified as the most common and/or most destructive negative police/citizen encounters. Plan your presentation as if it were to be given to young police officers as they begin their careers, your overall objectives being to prevent these young officers from ever creating or contributing to the creation of the kind of negative police encounters your group is presenting.

Because your purpose is to have a profound, lasting impact on behavior, your method of presentation may extend beyond lecture and discussion. Application of the dramatic and other arts is encouraged.

HUMAN DIGNITY: NEGATIVE EXPERIENCE IN THE POLICE ORGANIZATION

Please reflect on your experience in the police organization and describe to your partner for this exercise the personal experience in which you felt that your human dignity was violated—you were insulted, disrespected, treated unjustly, unnecessarily physically endangered—BY THE POLICE ORGANIZATION.

• Please discuss your negative experience in the police organization and the negative experiences of the others in the group.

• Please identify three or four incidents or situations that exemplify the most common, most frequent and most destructive negative encounters or experiences that police have within the police organization. These situations may be drawn directly from specific personal experiences discussed in the group or based more generally on the group's discussion of negative experiences in the organization.

• Please work with your group to develop ways to present to our entire assembly of course participants the three or four experiences your group has identified as the most common and/or most destructive negative experiences in the police organization. Plan your presentation as if it were to be given to young police officers as they begin their careers. Your overall objective being two-fold: (1) to protect these young officers by preparing them for potentially negative experiences; and (2) to prevent them from ever creating or contributing to the creation of the kind of negative police/police encounters your group is presenting.

Because your purpose is to have a profound, lasting impact on behavior your method of presentation may extend beyond lecture and discussion. Application of the dramatic and other arts is encouraged.

HUMAN DIGNITY: GROUP COMMUNICATION AND ACHIEVEMENT EXERCISE

You are asked to participate in a group communication exercise, the rules of which are:

• Members of the Blue group can send two messages (an X or a Y) to the Green group.

• Members of the Green group can send two messages (an A or a B) to the Blue group.

The results of the exchange of messages is as follows:

If the Blues send *and*	the Greens send	then the results are:
X	B	the Blues gain 15 points
		the Greens gain 0 points
Y	A	the Blues gain 0 points
		the Greens gain 15 points
Y	B	the Blues gain 5 points
		the Greens gain 5 points
X	A	the Blues gain 0 points
		the Greens gain 0 points

The groups will meet separately and communicate with each other only through the letter messages A, B, X, Y, as described above and through the authorized emissaries (the trainers).

This portion of the exercise will take one to two hours.

The goal of the exercise is to earn as many points for your group as possible.

Sample letter cards appear below:

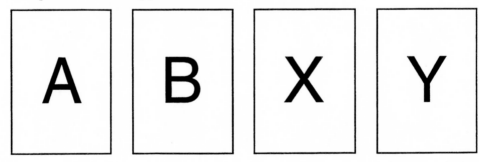

HUMAN DIGNITY IN POLICING: EQUAL PROTECTION FOR ALL, INCLUDING SOCIETY'S OUTCASTS

While it is generally agreed that all persons deserve equal treatment under the law, as a professional police officer, you must deal with the reality that some people or some groups of people are more at risk than others in encounters with the police.

Now we're asking you to serve on a police agency committee charged with the task of protecting the human dignity of society's deviant or outcast groups.

Your committee has divided into subgroups and your subgroup is assigned to report on one particular deviant or outcast group. Each subgroup should identify an outcast group or subgroup and give a brief presentation (5 to 10 minutes) to the committee (all course participants) as a whole that will include discussion of:

• Who the outcast group is and why they are who they are.

• How they feel about themselves and others in society including the police.

• What police policies, procedures, supervisors, or training approaches might be necessary in order to better protect the human dignity of the group.

PROFESSIONAL ETHICS IN POLICE WORK

The case studies which follow, presented to the training group, illustrate ethical issues or questions that commonly confront police.

Please meet with your group in order to:

• Identify the ethical problem or issue or question illustrated in the case study and

• Design an appropriate police agency strategy (recruitment, selection, training, supervision, internal investigation, etc.) in response to the ethical problem or issue or question.

Incident 1

A police detective delivering money to ransom the teenage daughter of a wealthy family manages to apprehend the alleged kidnapper after a violent encounter that leaves both the detective and the kidnap suspect wounded. According to the perpetrator's original ransom demand, the victim is buried and her life is dependent on a mechanically operated air supply that will run out of fuel and cease to operate in a few hours. Because of the time pressure, the detective immediately begins interrogation of the suspect regarding the whereabouts of the kidnapped young woman.

The suspect tells the detective that he knows that the police have enough evidence to convict him of kidnapping and that he expects to be sent to prison for the rest of his life. He also says that he will not tell them where the kidnapped girl is buried because he has nothing more to lose, and does not want to give police the satisfaction of rescuing her. He then asks for drugs to relieve his pain and to put him to sleep so that he isn't bothered any longer by the detective's questions.

What ethical issues confront the detective involved in this case?

What issue or issues does the case raise for police supervisors, police managers, and the police organization?

Incident 2

After being assaulted, disarmed, and shot at with his own weapon, a police officer, dazed but otherwise not seriously injured, chases and corners his assailant on a deserted pier. It is late at night, there are no bystanders, and the officer, away from his vehicle and without a hand-held radio, can't expect backup from other officers because he can't call for help.

Having counted the shots fired at him, the officer knows that his gun, which is still in the perpetrator's hands, is now empty. Armed with a makeshift weapon he has picked up during the chase, the officer moves in to capture his assailant. Once again, the perpetrator tries to shoot the officer but upon discovering that the gun is empty, he meekly submits, telling the officer that he is now unarmed and willing to be taken into custody.

What ethical issue or issues confront the police officer involved in this case?

What issue or issues does the case raise for police supervisors, police managers, and the police organization?

Incident 3

A group of competent, honest police officers, who see themselves as protectors of society against violent crime, exploitation of the weak by the strong, etc., are dismayed by what they perceive to be subversion of the political and legal system by powerful and wealthy organized criminals.

The officers are outraged by a well-publicized case involving failure of the justice system to convict a notorious organized crime figure, who was charged with killing a labor union reformer and his entire family. Frustrated by what they perceive to be society's failure to achieve justice through legal means, the officers begin to employ intimidation, extortion and even homicide in order to fight organized criminals.

What ethical issue or issues confront the police officers involved in this case?
What issue or issues does the case raise for police supervisors, police managers, and the police organization?

Incident 4

An undercover officer who has managed to infiltrate a notorious gang, to the point where he has been accepted as a member, is told to "punish" a delinquent debtor of the gang leader. He is told where the debtor is to be found, and ordered to bring back a finger as evidence that the job has been done. The officer knows that if he refuses, his cover will be blown or he himself will be "punished." If his cover is blown, the authorities will lose their only real opportunity to bring many of the gang members to justice. On the other hand, if he inflicts the beating and severs the finger, he will be acting illegally and presumably, immorally.

What should the officer do?

Incident 5

You are a police district commander. Your government has decided to construct a large medical facility in the jurisdiction where you are commander of police. You were appointed to a large committee of government officials who serve as an advisory board for this project.

Several multinational construction corporations have contacted the government seeking the contract to construct the facility. Representatives of one of these corporations contacts you and asks you to do anything you can do to get them the contract. You are not permitted to tell them, but you know that the decision has already been made to award the contract to their organization.

The construction company representatives continue saying that, in return for your help, they will totally renovate the police district headquarters which is adjacent to the site where the proposed medical facility will be constructed. This renovation, which is needed, will be done free of charge, with workers on down-time and with surplus materials from the medical facility project nearby. The construction corporation representatives also indicate that upon completion of the medical construction project, several four-wheel drive vehicles that the company plans to use to transport supervisory personnel at the site will be turned over, again free of charge, to the police department, where such vehicles are badly needed.

What course of action should be taken by the police commander in the situation described above?
Why should the commander take this course of action?

Incident 6

You are a district police commander. A legitimate citizen, owner of a small but very successful restaurant, and well known in the community, is in police custody charged with a relatively minor offense. At worst, the offender will be required to pay a fine, which he can readily afford. In such cases, it is normally the practice of the police to schedule the offender to appear in court in the near future and to release him from custody. In this case, however, the investigating officer recommends that the individual be held in jail until the case is heard by the court. This is a legal but unusual course of action given the circumstances. When asked why he wants to hold the man, the investigating officer reports that several months earlier the accused was the victim of a serious assault. The investigator believes that the assault is related to an attempt by members of an organized criminal enterprise to extort money and gain control of legitimate businesses in the area.

The man in custody, according to the investigating officer, was totally uncooperative when interviewed by police investigating the assault and suspected extortion that occurred several months earlier. The investigating officer goes on to speculate that this individual whose testimony against his assailant could open the door to prosecution of members of an important organized crime group may decide to cooperate with the police if he shares a jail cell with some of society's less desirable deviants. The typical jail occupant, unfortunately, is likely to be assaultive and many are suffering from one or more serious communicable diseases. The investigator indicates that this is the only, perfectly legal way that he knows of to effectively encourage the individual in custody to help the police to deal with organized crime's invasion of the legitimate marketplace. They (organized criminals), the investigator says, are better equipped and financed than the police are and, in this case, because of fortuitous circumstances, police have a rare chance to fight back and can't let it just pass by.

What action do you take in this case?
Why do you take this course of action?

PROFESSIONAL ETHICS: THE MOST DIFFICULT DECISIONS

Please reflect on your police career and identify the most difficult ethical decision you've ever had to make.

Now, turn to the person next to you with whom you are paired for this exercise and tell your partner about the experience including the situation, the decision you made, your reasons for what you did, and the impact it had on you.

Please also be prepared to share your experience with our group as a whole.

IMPLEMENTING A CODE OF CONDUCT: MAKING RESPECT FOR HUMAN DIGNITY LIVE IN THE DAY-TO-DAY OPERATION OF A POLICE AGENCY

Without in any way seeking to diminish the value of codes of conduct for police, it is important to note that whether or not a code of conduct or some other mandate to respect human dignity has real impact depends most critically on the steps an agency takes to enforce its rules of conduct or to carry out its mandate in practice.

You are asked, therefore, to help your chief executive officer prepare for a major press conference at which he or she will be asked to describe in detail the ways in which your agency's commitment to human dignity (as reflected in its public statements, its written procedures and codes, and most recently, its participation in this Human Dignity course) is implemented operationally.

Because this is a formidable task, the work is divided among subgroups:

• A group on training that will describe how the agency's commitment to human dignity is implemented in training of both entry level and experienced personnel.

• A group on frontline supervision that will describe how the agency's commitment to human dignity is implemented in supervisory policy and supervisory practices.

• A group on midlevel management that will describe how the agency's commitment to human dignity is implemented by police area field commanders.

• A group on citizen complaints that will describe how the agency's commitment to human dignity is implemented in responding to allegations of police misconduct.

UNITED NATIONS CODE OF CONDUCT FOR LAW ENFORCEMENT OFFICIALS

Law enforcement officials shall at all times fulfill the duty imposed upon them by law, by serving the community and by protecting all persons against illegal acts, consistent with the high degree of responsibility required by their profession.

In the performance of their duty, law enforcement officials shall respect and protect human dignity and maintain and uphold the human rights of all persons.

Law enforcement officials may use force only when strictly necessary and to the extent required for the performance of their duty.

Matters of a confidential nature in the possession of law enforcement officials shall be kept confidential, unless the performance of duty or the needs of justice strictly require otherwise.

No law enforcement official may inflict, instigate or tolerate any act of torture or other cruel, inhuman or degrading treatment or punishment, nor may any law enforcement official invoke superior orders or exceptional circumstances such as a state of war or a threat of war, a threat to national security, internal political instability or any other public emergency as a justification of torture or other cruel, inhuman or degrading treatment or punishment.

Law enforcement officials shall ensure the full protection of the health of persons in their custody and, in particular, shall take immediate action to secure medical attention whenever required.

Law enforcement officials shall not commit any act of corruption. They shall also rigorously oppose and combat all such acts.

Law enforcement officials shall respect the law and the present Code. They shall also, to the best of their capability, prevent and rigorously oppose any violations of them.

Law enforcement officials who have reason to believe that a violation of the present Code has occurred or is about to occur shall report the matter to their superior authorities and, where necessary, to other appropriate authorities or organs vested with reviewing or remedial power.

Appendix B

REPORT ON THE JUNE WORKSHOP: AN ELECTRONIC INTERACTIVE SURVEY OF POLICE OFFICIALS FROM SOUTH AND CENTRAL AMERICA AND THE CARIBBEAN ON THE SUBJECT OF HUMAN DIGNITY*

QUESTIONNAIRE AND RESPONSE TOTALS
THE HUMAN DIGNITY PROGRAM

1. Let's begin by having everyone identify where they are from.
    1. Caribbean — 21%
    2. Central America — 52%
    3. South America — 26%
    4. North America — —

2. Now, please tell me how long you have been in police work.
    1. Less than 10 years — 21%
    2. 10-20 years — 26%
    3. Over 20 years — 52%

3. Have you ever been a victim of a crime?
    1. Yes — 56%
    2. No — 44%

4. Have you ever been shot at or wounded?
    1. Yes — 42%
    2. No — 58%

---

* Conducted by Rowan and Michaels in cooperation with John Jay College of Criminal Justice City University of New York and ICITAP, June 15, 1992

4.1. Does being the victim of crime, or shot at, make someone:
    1. A better police officer   77%
    2. A worse police officer   -
    3. No different   23%

4.2 In your experience, have you ever used victims of crime to tell their stories to police as part of police training?
    1. Yes   40%
    2. No   60%

4.3 Would it be a good idea to use victims in the training of police?
    1. Yes   79%
    2. No   21%

5. Have you been the object of discrimination or prejudice?
    1. Yes   47%
    2. No   53%

5.1 Does your agency, or the agencies you work with have a counseling department?
    1. Yes   56%
    2. No   44%

5.2 Should there be a counseling department at your agency?
    1. Yes   100%
    2. No   --

5.3 Is there a psychological exam in your police training programs?
    1. Yes   79%
    2. No   21%

6. Is discrimination by the police a major or minor problem where you live?
    1. Major   47%
    2. Minor   47%
    3. Not a problem at all   6%

7. How much prejudice exists among police officers where you work?
    1. A lot   33%
    2. Some   27%
    3. A little   40%
    4. None   --

8. Is violent, interpersonal crime, and brutality in your country –
  1. Increasing?   77%
  2. Decreasing?   23%

9. The disappearances of people who are known to have been in contact with the criminal justice system are:
  1. Rare-unusual   94%
  2. Frequent enough to be disturbing   –
  3. Common   6%

10. Deaths of people in custody of the police are:
  1. Rare-unusual   82%
  2. Frequent enough to be disturbing   12%
  3. Common   6%

11. Police use of excessive force in arrests and interrogations is:
  1. Rare-unusual   41%
  2. Frequent enough to be disturbing   47%
  3. Common   12%

12. Have you, yourself, ever witnessed a police situation in which excessive force was used?
  1. Yes   83%
  2. No   17%

13. Does experience with violent situations produce a dehumanizing effect in the police officer's life or with his family? In other words, to what extent are officers brutalized by overexposure to violent situations and thereby out of touch with their own likes and feelings?
  1. To a significant extent   12%
  2. Somewhat   47%
  3. Not very much   41%

14. Does overexposure to violent situations play an important role in causing police officers to act first, before thinking about alternatives or before fully analyzing situations?
  1. Happens a lot   22%
  2. Happens sometimes   61%
  3. Happens very rarely   17%

15. In general, is it your experience that all people are treated fairly by the police, or do some people get treated significantly better than others, for whatever reason?

1. All are treated fairly	11%
2. Some are treated better than others	89%

16. How much respect does the typical police officer have for the court system?

1. A great deal	50%
2. Relatively little	50%

17. Which of the following methods would be more effective in reducing the amount of criminal behavior in your society?

1. Create more external controls, such as more police, prisons and stiffer sentences, or	6%
2. Create more economic opportunity, such as jobs for the population in general	94%

17.1 Are the politicians in your country making a sincere effort to provide economic opportunity to the population at-large?

1. Yes	44%
2. No	56%

18. How many prisoners are helped or rehabilitated in prison?

1. Many	–
2. Some	25%
3. Few	56%
4. None	19%

18.1 In your opinion, should prisons rehabilitate prisoners?

1. Yes	94%
2. No	6%

18.2 Do you have personal knowledge of prison rehabilitation–a real experience?

1. Yes	56%
2. No	44%

19. Does the public support your police agency or the agencies you work with?

1. Most of the time	41%
2. Some of the time	41%
3. Rarely	18%

20. How often is your police agency, or the agencies you work with, the target of public criticism or anger?

1. Often	70%
2. Sometimes	24%
3. Rarely	6%

21. Does the news media generally treat your police agency or the agencies you work with –

1. Fairly?	39%
2. Unfairly?	61%

22. In your experience, does the average citizen generally respect or fear the police?

1. Respect	29%
2. Fear	71%

23. Do you think that human dignity changes fundamentally from culture to culture, or do you believe that human dignity is a universal concept applicable to all conditions and cultures of the world?

1. It varies greatly depending on culture and other conditions	18%
2. It is universal and unchanging	82%

24. Do you think the exercise you've just completed was:

1. An effective way to get into the discussion	100%
2. Just one of many ways of conducting the discussion–nothing special	–

25. Is fear a useful means of controlling the public?

1. Very	7%
2. Somewhat	29%
3. Not useful	64%

Appendix C

INTERNATIONAL LAW ENFORCEMENT ACADEMY SESSION EVALUATION DATA SUMMARIES

SESSION 98-18

Evaluation #: 981811   **Instructor: Tricomi-Higgins, Donato**
Course Name: Human Dignity   **Agency: JJCC**

	Bulgaria	Georgia	Hungary	Student Average
1. The instructor had knowledge and experience in this area.	5.0	4.9	5.0	5.0
2. The instructor addressed our content/skill needs and interests.	4.7	5.0	4.7	4.8
3. The instructor answered our questions effectively.	4.8	4.8	4.7	4.8
4. The instructor provided the class with course goals and objectives.	4.8	5.0	4.7	4.8
5. The instructor effectively achieved the course goals and objectives.	4.7	4.8	4.9	4.8
6. The instructor included learning activities which actively involved the students.	4.8	5.0	4.7	4.8
7. The session was well organized.	4.9	4.9	4.6	4.8

150

	Bulgaria	Georgia	Hungary	Student Average
8. The information/skill learned in this class is useful and could be applied to my work now.	4.6	4.9	4.1	4.5
9. The information/skill learned in this class may help me in my future work.	4.6	4.9	4.3	4.6
10. The session was intellectually challenging.	4.6	4.8	4.2	4.5
11. The handout materials and the audio visuals were informative.	4.6	4.6	4.2	4.5
12. The written materials were clear and easy to understand.	4.6	4.8	4.2	4.5
13. The interpretation provided was clear and understandable.	5.0	5.0	5.0	5.0
14. I learned new information in this course.	4.6	4.8	4.4	4.6
15. Overall, this course was interesting.	4.8	4.9	4.6	4.8
16. Overall, the instructor was effective.	4.9	4.9	4.9	4.9
17. Overall, this course was valuable and the time was well spent.	4.9	5.0	4.6	4.8
18. I would recommend this course for future ILEA Programs.	4.8	4.9	4.6	4.8
OVERALL SESSION RATING:	4.8	4.9	4.6	4.7

SESSION 98-16

Evaluation #: 981611   Instructor: C. Tricomi-Higgins, Robert Donato
Course Name: Human Dignity   Agency: JJCC

	Kyrgyzstan	Moldova	Ukraine	Student Average
1. The instructor had knowledge and experience in this area.	5	5	5	5.0
2. The instructor addressed our content/skill needs and interests.	5	5	5	5.0
3. The instructor answered our questions effectively.	4.9	5	5	5.0
4. The instructor provided the class with course goals and objectives.	4.9	5	4.9	5.0
5. The instructor effectively achieved the course goals and objectives.	4.9	4.9	5	4.9
6. The instructor included learning activities which actively involved the students.	4.9	4.9	5	5.0
7. The session was well organized.	5	5	5	5.0
8. The information/skill learned in this class is useful and could be applied to my work now.	4.9	5	4.8	4.9
9. The information/skill learned in this class may help me in my future work.	5	5	4.9	5.0
10. The session was intellectually challenging.	5	4.9	4.9	5.0
11. The handout materials and the audio visuals were informative.	5	4.9	4.9	4.9
12. The written materials were clear and easy to understand.	4.9	4.9	4.9	4.9

	Kyrgyzstan	Moldova	Ukraine	Student Average
13. The interpretation provided was clear and understandable.	5	5	5	5.0
14. I learned new information in this course.	5	5	4.9	5.0
15. Overall, this course was interesting.	4.9	5	4.9	5.0
16. Overall, the instructor was effective.	5	5	5	5.0
17. Overall, this course was valuable and the time was well spent.	5	5	4.9	5.0
18. I would recommend this course for future ILEA Programs.	4.9	5	4.9	4.9
OVERALL SESSION RATING:	4.9	4.9	4.9	5.0

SESSION 96-8

Evaluation #:9681109
Course Name: Human Dignity

Instructor: Pitt & Anderson
Agency: John Jay

	Croatia	Hungary	Macedonia	Average
1. The instructor had knowledge and experience in this area.	4.9	4.9	4.8	4.9
2. The instructor addressed our content/skill needs and interests.	4.9	4.9	5.0	4.9
3. The instructor answered our questions effectively.	4.9	4.9	4.8	4.9
4. The instructor provided the class with course goals and objectives.	4.8	4.9	4.9	4.9
5. The instructor effectively achieved the course goals and objectives.	4.9	4.9	4.9	4.9

	Croatia	Hungary	Macedonia	Average
6. The instructor included learning activities which actively involved the students.	5.0	4.9	4.9	4.9
7. The session was well organized.	5.0	4.9	4.9	4.9
8. The information/skill learned in this class is useful and could be applied to my work now.	4.6	4.6	4.6	4.6
9. The information/skill learned in this class may help me in my future work.	4.6	4.6	4.8	4.7
10. The session was intellectually challenging.	4.9	4.8	5.0	4.9
11. The handout materials and the audio visuals were informative.	4.9	4.6	4.8	4.7
12. The written materials were clear and easy to understand.	4.8	4.7	4.8	4.8
13. The interpretation provided was clear and understandable.	4.9	4.9	4.9	4.9
14. I learned new information in this course.	4.8	4.8	4.8	4.8
15. Overall, this course was interesting.	4.9	5.0	4.9	4.9
16. Overall, the instructor was effective.	4.9	4.9	4.9	4.9
17. Overall, this course was valuable and the time was well spent	4.8	4.9	5.0	4.9
18. I would recommend this course for future ILEA programs.	4.9	5.0	5.0	5.0
OVERALL SESSION RATING:	4.9	4.8	4.9	4.9

Appendix D

AN ASSESSMENT OF THE IMPACT OF THE HUMAN DIGNITY COURSE

RAYMOND PITT, PH.D.

AREAS IMPACTED BY THE HUMAN DIGNITY AND THE POLICE COURSE:

A. Professional Attitudes

1. Greater feeling of professionalism, a new connection to their work, a new way to measure their effectiveness, greater feeling of efficiency, and sense of control.

2. Increased interest in human rights, listening skills, dealing with the mentally ill.

B. Professional Skills

1. Listening
2. Communicating
3. Empathizing
4. Participating in discussions

C. Policies And Practices

1. Prisoner's needs—bail, relatives, clean facilities, reduced time, communicating with prisoners—inmate culture improved.
2. Civilian contacts in the ghettos—improved communication, like community policing.
3. Youth programs
4. High school presentations

5. Treatment of subordinates–listening, communicating, less punishment, more help to officers.
6. Civilian complaints

D. Personal Relationships

1. A new feeling of competence, capability, and well-being, and for some, being reborn.
2. Better interaction with spouse and children, more listening, better communicating, less impatience, criticism, or harshness.
3. Greater awareness that everyone is a human being deserving of respect for their human dignity.
4. They now know what to listen for when dealing with people.

E. Continuing Needs

1. Although superiors tend to support them, they want to get additional training.
2. They want to learn how to communicate criticism up the hierarchy.
3. They would like more training in listening, and in managing mentally ill clients.
4. They feel that they have helped to develop this course for themselves; they would like to have additional copies of course outlines, handouts, etc.

COURSE IMPACT AS REPORTED BY PARTICIPATING OFFICERS

A. Impact on Professional Life

All officers stated that the course had a real impact on them, both professionally and personally. They noted the following:

1. They felt a great professionalism in their work as well as greater efficiency and feeling of well-being.

2. Some reported that they now had a way of assessing themselves at the end of each day in terms of not having violated anyone's human dignity.

3. All reported an increased ability to communicate with subordinates, peers, civilians, and where applicable, with criminal elements and prisoners.

4. Equally important, they reported an increased ability to listen to subordinates, peers, civilians, prisoners, etc. They now saw and heard so much more in their interactions with people because they knew what to listen and look for.

5. For many police, the experience of the course was a profound enlightenment which took the following forms:

• The ability to identify with others as human beings having the same or similar feelings as they did and deserving the right to equal and fair treatment.

• The development of a new way of relating to subordinates, peers and civilians, prisoners, etc. This new way of relating was a composite of respect for human dignity, the awareness of the humanity and feelings of the others, and the right of every person to fair and equal treatment.

• The feeling on their return to work that something special had happened to them. They were born again, renewed, had a new vision and they showed this new feeling and capability with their peers, superiors, and subordinates.

B. Impact on Family Life

1. Many officers reported that their family life improved as a consequence of the training. For some, it was a better relationship with their spouse and children. What had improved was their ability to listen and avoid negative statements that would have resulted in the usual arguments.

2. The officers noted that the improvement in their home life had a positive effect on their job performance. Of interest–officers who identified themselves as Christians did not experience as much of a change in their personal lives as they had in their professional lives. However, they felt the course reinforced the respect with which they related to their families.

C. Implementation

The change of attitude, the change of personal perspective, the ability to relate in a new way, the vision of all people as deserving of respect for their human dignity, the new ability to listen and communicate, and their commitment to implement the ideals of the course all played a part in the actual implementation that occurred. Following is a list of what officers did.

1. All officers responsible for prisoners made great efforts to improve the conditions of the holding cells and the expeditious and decent treatment of prisoners. Prisoners' complaints and needs were listened to for the first time, resulting in less time in confinement, earlier bail hearings, more visits from relatives, and better inmate/officer interaction; latrines were cleaned up as

well. All officers reported that prisoners responded most favorably to the change in attitude so much so that incidents declined almost to none and the entire atmosphere of the holding areas changed in a positive way, making the officers actually enjoy their work.

2. Positive contact with civilians in the ghettos increased dramatically. The positive attitude, interest in, and listening to their needs resulted in an approach that we call community policing.

3. New methods were instituted to collect and act on community complaints. Police officers reported civilians being very appreciative of the new approach.

4. Many officers reported reaching out for the first time to youth groups and helping youth programs in their community.

5. Many officers now made visits to schools to talk about human dignity issues.

6. One officer developed a relationship with a mental hospital in dealing with the hospitalization of a prisoner.

7. A significant area of change was the way officers now treated their subordinates.

• They listened more to their problems.

• They tended to use punishment less and instead tried to find solutions.

• They found their authority with their officers increased as a result of these new approaches. Officers whom they had disliked considered human dignity an eye-opener. They never had a course like this before. The openness and sharing exposed them to each person's feelings and history, i.e., their humanity. The discussions fostered a democratic spirit of exploration rather than a teacher-student model.

• This aspect of the course, rapping and explaining, sharing and listening, provided the officers with new tools to conduct the training of their subordinates which many officers employed for the first time. Many had group discussions rather than lectures and one trainer actually asked his students to recount violations of their human dignity.

• A number of officers wanted additional training in listening skills. A number also wanted more training in managing mentally ill patients. They also wanted their superiors to get training in human dignity or at least learn the basic objectives of the course. The one career issue that might be developed into a scenario had to do with how a junior officer can offer advice or even criticism to a superior officer. Also, they wanted more materials on human rights.

• Finally, the most significant impression to me was that these officers realized that they had developed the course for themselves and were fully responsible for propagating and developing it further. They may need help in starting a newsletter or developing training materials, but they are really off and running and implementing it.

BIBLIOGRAPHY

1987: A retrospective. (1987, January 26). *Law Enforcement News*, p. 3.

Aitchison, W. (1990). *The rights of law enforcement officers*. Portland, OR: Labor Relations Information Systems.

Alderson, J. (1984). *Human rights and the police*. Strasbourg: Council of Europe.

Andreopoulos, G. J., & Claude, R. P. (Eds.). (1997). *Human rights education for the twenty-first century*. Philadelphia: University of Pennsylvania Press.

Applbaum, A. (1995). Professional detachment: The executioner of Paris. *Harvard Law Review, 109*(2), 458-486.

Bayley, D. H. (1994). *Police for the future*. New York: Oxford University Press.

Bayley, D. H., & Shearing, C. D. (1996). The future of policing. *Law and Society Review, 30*(3), 585-607.

Berkley, G. E. (1969). *The democratic policeman*. Boston: Beacon Press.

Bizzack, J. W. (Ed.). (1991). *Issues in policing: New perspectives*. Lexington, KY: Autumn House.

Bouza, A. V. (1991). The police and the press. In J.W. Bizzack (Ed.), *Issues in policing: New perspectives*. Lexington, KY: Autumn House.

Bouza, A. V., & Sherman, L. W. (1991). Controlling police wrongdoing. In J.W. Bizzack (Ed.), Issues in policing: New perspectives. Lexington, KY: Autumn House.

Brann, J. E., & Whalley, S. (1992). *COPPS: The transformation of police organizations* (Community Oriented Policing and Problem Solving). Sacramento, CA: California Attorney General's Crime Prevention Center.

Brockett, R. G. (Ed.). (1988). *Ethical issues in adult education*. New York: Teachers College Press.

Brookfield, S. D. (1986). *Understanding and facilitating adult learning*. San Francisco: Jossey-Bass.

Brookfield, S. D. (1987). *Developing critical thinkers: Challenging adults to explore alternative ways of thinking and acting*. San Francisco: Jossey-Bass.

Bumphus, V. (1991). *Civilian review of the police: The 50 largest cities, 1991*. Omaha, NE: Department of Criminal Justice, Nebraska.

Burden, P. (1981). The business of crime reporting: Problems and dilemmas. In C. Sumner (Ed.), *Crime, justice and the mass media: Papers presented to the 14th Cropwood Conference 1981*. Cambridge, England: Institute of Criminology.

Burnham, D. (1977). *The role of the media in controlling corruption*. New York: John Jay Press.

Cahill, T. (1998). *The gifts of the Jews: How a tribe of desert nomads changed the way everyone thinks and feels*. New York: Doubleday.

Cell, E. (1984). *Learning to learn from experience.* Albany, NY: State University of New York Press.

Cohen, H. S., & Feldberg, M. (1984). *Power and restraint: The moral dimension of police work.* New York: Praeger.

Cole, G.F., Frankowski, S.J., & Gertz, M.G. (1987). *Major criminal justice systems.* Newbury Park, CA: Sage.

Dales, R. C. (1979). A medieval view of human dignity. *Journal of the History of Ideas, 38*(4), 557-559.

Delattre, E. J. (1989). *Character and cops: Ethics in policing.* Washington, DC: AEI Press.

Delattre, E. J. (1991). *Character and cops: Ethics in policing* (3rd ed.). Washington, DC: AEI Press.

Elias, J. L., & Merriam, S. (1980). *Philosophical foundations of adult education.* Malabar, FL: Robert E. Kreiger.

Elliston, F. A., & Feldberg, M. (1985). *Moral issues in police work.* Totowa, NJ: Rowman and Allanheld.

Flanagan, T. J., & Longmire, D. R. (Eds.). (1996). *Americans view crime and justice: A national public opinion survey.* Thousand Oaks, CA: Sage.

Flanagan, T. J., & Vaughn, M. S. (1992). Public opinion about police abuse of force. In W.A. Geller and H. Toch (Eds.), *And justice for all: Understanding and controlling police abuse of force.* Washington, DC: Police Executive Research Forum.

For now, no names mentioned in dispute over police-abuse files. (1996, September 15). *Law Enforcement News,* p. 1.

Gaffigan, S. J., & McDonald, P. P. (1997). *Police integrity: Public service with honor.* Washington, DC: U.S. Department of Justice.

Gates, D. F. (1992). *Chief: My life in the LAPD.* New York: Bantam.

Geller, W. A., & Toch, H. (Eds.). (1995). *And justice for all: Understanding and controlling police abuse of force.* Washington, DC: Police Executive Research Forum.

Goldstein, H. (1990). *Problem-Oriented policing.* New York: McGraw Hill.

Goldstein, H. (1993). *The new policing: Confronting complexity* (Research in Brief). Washington, DC: U.S. Department of Justice, National Institute of Justice.

Heffernan, W. C., & Stroup, T. (1985). *Police ethics: Hard choices in law enforcement.* New York: John Jay Press.

Huang, W. S. Wilson, & Vaughn, M. S. (1996). Support and confidence: Public attitudes toward the police. In T.J. Flanagan and D.R. Longmire (Eds.), *Americans view crime and justice: A national public opinion survey.* Thousand Oaks, CA: Sage.

Jarvis, P. (1987). *Adult learning in the social context.* London: Croom Helm.

Jeffers, H. P. (1994). *Commissioner Roosevelt: The story of Theodore Roosevelt and the New York City Police, 1895-1897.* New York: John Wiley & Sons.

Jones v. Marshall, 528 F. 2d. (C.A. 2 1975).

Kant, I. (1963). *Groundwork of the metaphysic of morals.* (H.J. Paton, Trans.). New York: Barnes & Noble. (Original work published in 1785).

Kappeler, V. E., Sluder, R. D., & Alpert, G. P. (1994). *Forces of deviance: Understanding the dark side of policing.* Prospect Heights, IL: Waveland Press.

Kelling, G. L. (1988). *The evolving strategy of policing.* Washington, DC: U.S. Department of Justice, National Institute of Justice.

Kelling, G. L., Wasserman, R., & Williams, H. (1988). *Police accountability and community policing.* Washington, DC: U.S. Department of Justice, National Institute of Justice.

Kelly, P. (1991). The media and the police: Contemporary experiments in cross-education. In J.W. Bizzack (Ed.), *Issues in policing: New perspectives.* Lexington, KY: Autumn House.

Kennedy, W. B. (1990). Integrating personal and social ideologies. In J. Mezirow and Associates, *Fostering critical reflection in adulthood: A study guide to transformative and emancipatory learning.* San Francisco: Jossey-Bass.

Kleinig, J. (1996). *The ethics of policing.* New York: Cambridge University Press.

Kleinig, J. with Zhang, Y. (Comps. & Eds.). (1993). *Professional law enforcement codes: A documentary collection.* Westport, CT: Greenwood Press.

Knox, A. B. (1993). *Strengthening adult and continuing education: A global perspective on synergistic leadership.* San Francisco: Jossey-Bass.

Kobel, R. (1988, July). The pen vs. the sword: Do police determine the rules and tone of press relations?. *Law Enforcement News,* p. 1.

Kolb, D. A. (1984). *Experiential learning: Experience as the source of learning and development.* Englewood Cliffs, NJ: Prentice-Hall.

Koon, S. C., & Deitz, R. (1992). *Presumed guilty.* Washington, DC: Regnery Gateway.

Local government police management (3rd ed.). (1991). Washington, DC: International City Management Association.

Los Angeles CA Independent Commission on the Los Angeles Police Department. (1991). *Report* (Summary). Los Angeles, CA.

Maclaren, E. A. (1977). Dignity. *Journal of Medical Ethics, 3,* 40.

McAlary, M. (1994). *Good cop, bad cop.* New York: Pocket Books.

McEwen, T. (1996). *National data collection on police use of force.* Washington, DC: U.S. Department of Justice, Bureau of Justice Statistics.

Mezirow, J. (1990). How critical reflection triggers transformative learning. In J. Mezirow and Associates, *Fostering critical reflection in adulthood: A study guide to transformative and emancipatory learning.* San Francisco: Jossey-Bass.

Miller, L., & Braswell, M. (1983). *Human relations and police work.* Prospect Heights, IL: Waveland Press.

Misiak, H., & Sexton, V. S. (1973). *Phenomenological, existential and humanistic psychologies: A historical survey.* New York: Grune and Stratton.

Moore, M. A., & Stephens, D. W. (1991). *Beyond command and control. The strategic management of police departments.* Washington, DC: Police Executive Research Forum.

Municipal Management Series, Local Government Police Management (3rd ed.). (1991). Washington, DC: ICMA.

National Crime Prevention Council. (1994). *Working as partners with community groups.* Washington, DC: U.S. Department of Justice, Bureau of Justice Assistance.

Los Angeles CA Independent Commission on the Los Angeles Police Department. (1991). *Report* (Summary). Los Angeles, CA.

New York City Mayor's Commission to Investigate Allegations of Police Corruption. (1973). *The Knapp Commission report on police corruption.* New York: George Braziller.

New York, NY Commission to Investigate Allegations of Police Corruption. (1994). *Commission report.* New York, NY.

Oakley, R. B., Dziedzic, M. J., & Goldberg, E. M. (Eds.). (1998). *Policing the new world disorder: Peace operations and public security.* Washington, DC: National Defense University.

Overstreet, H. A. (1949). *The mature mind.* New York: Norton.

Owen, J. A. (1996). Character, deviance, and integrity in policing: A critical review of current literature. *Criminal Justice Review, 21*(2), 251-263.

Perez, D. W. (1992). Police review systems. *Management Information Service, 24*(8), 1-15.

Perez, D. W. (1994). *Common sense about police review.* Philadelphia: Temple University Press.

Pico della Mirandola, G. (1956). *Oration on the dignity of man.* (A.R. Caponigri, Trans.) Washington, DC: Regnery Gateway. (Original work published in 1496).

Prevention and control of urban disorders: Issues for the 1980's. (1980, October 27). *The Miami Herald,* p. 1B.

Right to privacy vs. public's right to know. (1997, May 15). *Law Enforcement News,* p. 7.

Rosen, M. S. (1993, January 15/31). 1992 in review: Eruptions, aftershocks and a shifting landscape. *Law Enforcement News,* p. 1.

Ross, J. I. (1993). *The politics and control of police violence in New York City and Toronto.* Unpublished doctoral dissertation, University Microfilms International, Ann Arbor, MI.

Rowe, P. J., & Whelan, C. J. (Eds.). (1985). *Military intervention in democratic societies.* London: Croom Helm Ltd.

Skolnick, J. H., & Fyfe, J. J. (1993). *Above the law.* New York: MacMillan Free Press.

Skolnick, J. H., & McCoy, C. (1985). Police accountability and the media. In W.A. Geller (Ed.), *Police leadership in America: Crisis and opportunity.* New York: Praeger.

Some complaints will disappear from California cops' personnel folders. (1996, November 15). *Law Enforcement News,* p. 1.

Sork, T. J. (1988). Ethical issues in program planning. In R.G. Brockett (Ed.), *Ethical issues in adult education.* New York: Teachers College Press.

Sumner, C. (Ed.). (1981). *Crime, justice and the mass media.* Cambridge: Institute of Criminology.

Surette, R. (1992). *Media, crime and criminal justice: Image and realities.* Belmont, CA: Brooks/Cole.

Toch, H., & Grant, J. D. (1991). *Police as problem solvers.* New York: Plenum.

Trojanowicz, R. C., & Bucqueroux, B. (1990). *Community policing.* Cincinnati, OH: Anderson.

Trojanowicz, R. C., & Bucqueroux, B. (1991). *Community policing and the challenge of diversity.* Washington, DC: U.S. Department of Justice, National Institute of Justice.

United Nations High Commissioner for Human Rights. (1997). *Human rights and law enforcement. A manual on human rights training for the police.* New York: United Nations.

U.S. Civil Rights Commission. (1981). *Who is guarding the guardians? A report on police practices.* Washington, DC: U.S. Government Printing Office.

U.S. Department of Justice, Law Enforcement Assistance Administration. (1980). *Prevention and control of urban disorders: Issues for the 1980's.* Washington, DC: University Research Corporation.

Walker, S., & Bumphus, V. W. (1991). Civilian review of the police: A national survey of the 50 largest cities. *Criminal Justice Police Focus, 91-93.*

Walsh, W. F., & Mannion, M. A. (1993). Law enforcement/media relations policy, training and attitudes: A perspective for the 1990s and beyond. *The Justice Journal, 8*(1), 86-107.

Wasserman, R., & Moore, M. H. (1988). *Values in policing.* Washington, DC: U.S. Department of Justice, National Institute of Justice.

Weinstein, G., & Fantini, M. D. (Eds.). (1970). *Toward humanistic education: A curriculum of affect.* New York: Praeger.

Wilson, J. Q., & Kelling, G. L. (1989). Making neighborhoods safe. *The Atlantic Monthly, 263*(2), 46-52.

Zhao, J. (1996). *Why police organizations change: A study of community-oriented policing.* Washington, DC: Police Executive Research Forum.

INDEX

A

American Bar Association, release of Reardon Report, 42

American Civil Liberties Union, Rhode Island affiliate role in suit *re* public disclosure of police brutality/misconduct complaints, 39

Anderson, David, editor at *New York Times*, 44

Anderson, McKee, "Human Dignity and The Police" trainer, x

Antigua, 105

Armstrong, Michael, 23

Aristotle, 55

Arizona *Republic*, 43

Association of Humanistic Psychology, 55

Austria, 105

B

Baltimore *Sun*, 34

Bergman, John, x

Berkeley Police Review Commission, 25

Bolivia, 88, 105

Bosnia, 105

Bouza, former Minneapolis Police Chief Anthony, 35, 39, 42, 44

Bratton, former NYC Commissioner William, 45-46, 116

Brown, former NYC Police Commissioner Lee, 23

Buda, 99

Budapest, 93, 95, 98-99

Bulgaria, 99

Bureau of Justice Statistics, 38

Burnham, David, *New York Times* reporter, 43

C

Cahill, Thomas, 55

Caiaphas Principle, 12

California, law on police misconduct complaint files, 39

Casillas, Yolanda, x

Chicago police, 1960s violence, 28

Christopher Commission (Independent Commission on the Los Angeles Police Department), 21-22, 26, 37

Civil action against police violations of rights, 32

Civil Rights Acts of 1871 and 1875, 30

Civil Rights Commission, US, Report of (1981), 31

Civil Rights Division, US Justice Department, 35

Civil War, US, 30

Clinton, US President William, 93

Cockburn, George, x

Colombia, works with ICITAP, 4, 88, 105

Columbia University, Graduate School of Journalism, 45; Teachers College, 76

Confederation, US Articles of, 30

Confucius, 55

Congress, US, 4

Constitution, US, Preamble, 3; 14th Amendment to, 29; 30

Corres, Rosemary, x

Costa Rica, 105

CNN, broadcast of Rodney King beating tape, 37

Criminal Justice Ethics, publication of John Jay College, 7

Cronkite, Walter, 45

Curran Commission, 115

Curran, James, director of "Human Dignity and The Police," x, xi, 101-02

Czech language, translations of, 101-02

Czech Republic, 100

Czechs, 100

D

Dade County, 19

Danube River, 99

Delattre, Edwin, police-press relations analyst, 41

Delgado, Sonya, x

Detroit, race riot during World War II, 16

Dewey Commission, 115

Dinkins, former NYC Mayor David, 23, 116

Dominican Republic, 105

Donato, Robert, x

Dowd, Michael, role in 1992 NYPD corruption scandal, 22, 24, 40

Drug Enforcement Administration, US, xi, 99

Durk, David, role in 1970 exposure of NYPD corruption, 41, 115

Dyncorp, 105

E

El Salvador, 88, 105, civil war in, 89

Estonia, 99

F

Federal Bureau of Investigation (FBI), US, xi, 26, 32, 92-95, 99; FBI Academy, 92-93, 98

Federal Law Enforcement Training Center (FLETC), xi, 105

Fernandez, Tom, x

Fiandaca, Cheryl, x

Field Force Concept, introduction of by Miami-Dade and Miami Police Departments, 20

Ft. Lauderdale Sun-Sentinel, 46

FMLN, 89

Frank, Anne, 66

Freedom of Information Act, 43

Freeh, FBI Director Louis J., 92, 98, 100

G

Gadsden, James, US Deputy Chief of Mission in Hungary, 100

Gandhi, 65

Garcia, Evelyn, x

Gates, former Los Angeles Police Chief Daryl F., 37

Giuliani, NYC Mayor Rudolph W., 46, 116

Goodman, Alan, x

Goodman, Don, x

Goncz, Hungarian President, 93

Grenada, 105

Guatemala, 105

H

Haiti, 110

Hatch, US Senator Orrin, 100

Hernandez-Miyares, Julio, x, 87, 101-02

Holliday, George, Rodney King beating tape, 21, 37

Hoover, J. Edgar, 113-14

Honduras, works with ICITAP, 4, 105, 108-09

House, California Assemblyman George, author of bill regarding citizen complaints against police, 39

Human dignity, title used instead of human rights, 5, 10; concept conforms to UN Code of Conduct for Law Enforcement Officials, 61

"Human Dignity and The Police,", development of course, ix, 5-7, 14; trust cornerstone of program, 26; founding of, 49-50; need for, 50-51; training methods, 52-53; philosophical basis, 53-56; input from participants, 56-59; training program, 61-64; program exercises, 64-74, 134-144; effect on attitudes of participants, 75-85; trainers' views, 86-90, 98-100, 102-03; first offered, 104; interactive surveys, 105-07, 145-59; end-of-course evaluations, 107-10, 112, 117; outline for trainees, including course goals and objectives, 122-26; manual for instructors, including instructional approaches and participant activities, 126-33; assessment of impact of course, 160-63

Humanist Manifesto (1933) and *Humanist Manifesto II* (1973), 55

Hungarian language, translations of, 101-02

Hungarian National Police, 96; National Police Training and Education Center, 93

Hungarians, 99

Hungary, 93, 96, 99, 105

I

International Association of Chiefs of Police (ICAP), 16, 38; discussion of public information policies, 42-43

International Criminal Investigation Training Assistance Program (ICITAP), 4-6, 54, 58-59, 94, 105-06, 108
International Curriculum Committee, 99
International Law Enforcement Academy (ILEA), 91-98; planning meeting, 99-100; putting plans into action, 100-03, 105, 108

J
Jairpersaud, Valerie, x
Jamaica, works with ICITAP, 4, 105; Jamaican police, 107-9
Jesus Christ, 65
John Jay College of Criminal Justice, ix, x, 5-6, 11, 14, 49-52, 57-58, 61, 76, 86, 94, 97-99, 106, 108; 30th anniversary of, 7
Johnson, Samuel, 13
Johnson, US President Lyndon B., 114
Jones, Seymour, x
Justice Department, US, 28, 32, 33; works with ICITAP, 4, 11; report on "Prevention and Control of Urban Disorders, Issues for the 1980s," 19; Civil Rights Division, 35
Juvenal, 3

K
Kant, Immanual, 11-13
Kefauver Commission, 1950s exposure of corruption, 16
Kennedy, William Bean, 77
King, Rev. Dr. Martin Luther Jr., 65
King, Rodney, beating incident, 16, 18-21, 28, 37-8, 46, 87, 111
Kleinig, John, x
Knapp Commission, "Report on Police Corruption" (1973), 17-8, 26, 43, 115
Koch, former NYC Mayor Edward, 116
Kriskovich, David "Kris," inspired "Human Dignity and The Police," x; Director of ICITAP, 4, 54, 87
KTLA-TV Channel 5, Los Angeles, 37

L
Lakhram, Ahalia, x
Latvia, 99
Law Enforcement News, publication of John Jay College, 7, 36, 39
Law Enforcement Education Program (LEEP), 114

Lexow Commission, 115
Liberty City disorders, 19
Lima, 87-8
Lincoln, Abraham, 65
Lindsay, former NYC Mayor John, 17
Lithuania, 99
Los Angeles *Daily News*, 37
Los Angeles disorders, 38, 87
Los Angeles Police Department, 21-2, 43; police scandal during World War II, 16
Los Angeles *Times*, 37
Lozano, Miami Police Officer William, 20
Louden, Bob, x
Lynch, Dr. Gerald W., President of John Jay College, 49, 95

M
Maclaren, Elizabeth, 1977 essay in *Journal of Medical Ethics*, 11
Madison, Wisconsin, suit *re* public access to citizen complaints against police, 39
Mandela, Nelson, 65
McCauley, David, x
McDuffie, Arthur, death at hands of Miami-Dade police officers, 18-19
Metro-Dade Police Department, 18-19; creates Citizens Advisory Committee, 20; Miami-Dade Police/Citizen Violence Reduction Project in wake of Liberty City disorders, 20
Mezirow, Jack, 76-77
Miami Police Department, 19-20
Middle States Association of Colleges and Universities, 98
Miller, John, former press aide at NYPD, 46
Mirandola, Giovanni Pico della, 11
Mollen Commission, 23, 26, 41, 115
Mollen, Milton, chair of commission to investigate corruption in NYPD, 23, 40, 115-116
Morrill Act (Land Grant Act of 1862), 112
Murphy, former NYPD Commissioner Patrick, 115

N
National Advisory Commission on Civil Disorders (Kerner Commission), 17
National Advisory Commission on Criminal Justice Standards and Goals (1973), 17

National Institute of Justice study on use of force, 47

National Opinion Survey on Crime and Justice (1995), 36

Nebraska, University of at Omaha, 1991 survey on civilian review of police, 25

New York *Daily News*, 36

New York Newsday, 36

New York *Times*, 41, 43-44

New York Police Department (NYPD), corruption in, 17, 23-24, 45-46, 86; Police Academy training, 59; 1997 brutality scandal, 111

Nicaragua, 105

Nieves, Mayra, x

O

Oklahoma City bombing, 100

P

Panama, 88, 105

Parker, Debra Hairston, x

Peel, Sir Robert, 113

Peru, works with ICITAP, 4; and Human Dignity course, 87-89, 105

Perez, Douglas, 24-25, 27

Pinter, Lt. Gen. Sandor, 93, 96, 99-100

Pitt, Ray, x, 80, 87, 101-02

Plato, 65

Poles, 99

Polish language, translations of, 101-02

Pledger, FBI Agent James, 98, 101

President's Commission on Campus Unrest (Kent State, 1970), 17

President's Commission on Causes and Prevention of Violence (1968), 17

President's Commission on Law Enforcement and the Administration of Justice (1967-68), 16

Price, Barbara, x

Providence, city of, 39

Puerto Rico Police Academy, 98

R

Reardon Report, 42

Reno, US Attorney General Janet, 100

Rhode Island, Supreme Court of rules on public disclosure of police brutality and discourtesy complaints, 39

Rodriguez, Carmen, x

Roosevelt, Theodore, former NYC Police Commissioner, 116; relationship with reporters when Commissioner, 45-46

Romania, 99

Ross, Jeffrey Ian, police scholar, 36; study of police violence in New York and Toronto, 39, 45

Roth, Richard, special assistant to former US Attorney General Thornburgh, 4

Rothlein, Mary DePiano, x, xi

Rowan, Mike, x

Russia, 99-100, 105

S

Safir, Howard, appointed NYC Police Commissioner, 46

St. Lucia, works with ICITAP, 4, 105

Sanson, Henri, 10

Seabury Commission, 115

Secret Service, US, 99

Serpico, Frank, 17, 41, 115

77th Precinct (Brooklyn), corruption scandal, 36, 39-40

Shining path guerrillas, 87

Sheppard v. Maxwell, US Supreme Court decision, 42

Sherman, Lawrence, 44

Simi Valley, California, 21

Slovakia, 99

State Department, US, 4, 108

Suffolk County (NY) Police Department, arrest of Michael Dowd, 24, 40

Surrette, Ray, 44

T

Tampa, Florida, site of 1980 trial in Arthur McDuffie case, 19

Taveras, John, x

Teresa, Mother, 65

Thomas, Gregory, x

Thornburgh, former US Attorney General Dick, 4

Treasury Department, US, 99; Federal Law Enforcement Training Center (FLETC) part of it, xi;

Tricomi-Higgins, Carolyn, x

Trimboli, NYPD Sgt. Joseph, 22, 40

U

Ukraine, 99-100

United States, adoption of English common law as criminal justice model, 29

United Nations Code of Conduct for Law Enforcement Officials, vii, 8-9, 14; "Human Dignity and The Police" designed to con form to, 14; text of, 144

United Nations peacekeeping mission in Haiti, 111

Universal Declaration of Human Rights, 14, 62, 101

V

Virginia Association of Chiefs of Police (VACOP), survey on use of force, 38

Virginia, University of, 93, 95, 99, 105

W

Ward, former NYC Police Commissioner Benjamin, 40

Wickersham Commission review of police misconduct (1931), 15

Willis, Kathy, x

Wisconsin, suit by newspapers for access to citizen complaints against police, 39

Wyllie, FBI Agent Terrie, 98

Y

Yoch, Marchelle, x